Victorian Woodturnings and Woodwork

THE 1893 BLUMER AND KUHN CATALOG OF PREMIUM MILLWORK

STAIRS, STAIR RAILINGS AND BALUSTERS, NEWEL POSTS, SPINDLES, MANTELS, ROSETTES, PLINTH AND HEAD BLOCKS, TURNED PORCH AND VERANDA WORK, GABLES, WINDOW HOODS, VENTILATORS, PEWS AND PULPITS, WOODEN ORNAMENTS, MOLDINGS AND INTERIOR FINISH, &C.

ASTRAGAL PRESS

Mendham, New Jersey

Library of Congress Catalog Card Number 95-77954
International Standard Book Number: 1-879335-67-0

Published by
The Astragal Press
5 Cold Hill Road, Suite #12
P.O. Box 239
Mendham, New Jersey 07945-0239

Printed in the United States of America

Introduction

In 1893, the Blumer & Kuhn Stair Co. of St. Louis, Missouri, had completed an expansion of its facilities, installed the latest and "most improved" machinery, and employed "only the Best" competent and skilled "workmen." With "great pleasure" the company presented "To the Trade" a copy of its new catalog with designs for its work.

Fortunately, at least one copy of the catalog has survived the intervening 100+ years. It is again with "great pleasure" that this unabridged reprint is presented "To the Trade," which today includes woodturners, cabinetmakers, furniture makers, architects, designers, hobbyists, house and furnishings restorers, &c.

Many of the designs illustrated in this book go well beyond the conventional examples of woodturning and woodworking commonly known for the period. It is these varied and unusual examples that make this collection so valuable.

Balusters

Balusters were one of the first items of elegance that were added to a structure to attract the eye and send a message of design excellence in the 1893 era.

Stair balusters were normally designed either 2 feet 4 inches or 2 feet 8 inches long, unless the design specifications required otherwise. These lengths would position handrails at the proper height. Where two balusters were used on each rise (step), the shorter length was installed near the front of the step with the longer length near the back.

With balusters, whether for interior use on steps and balconies or for exterior use on porches and railings, the design proportions dictated the aesthetic appeal of the construction. The good rule of proportions that they followed was to divide the total length into six portions. The length of the top detail and the base detail were one-half a portion each (one-twelfth). Where vase-like shapes were integral to the design, the widest point of the center shape was equal in width to the top and bottom and was positioned one-third up from the base. The narrowest part of the design was one-third down from the top and as small as one-third the width of the top.

Newel Posts and Stairs

The beginning, the end, and the corners of a well designed staircase should be accented with an elegant newel post. This design principle was well understood in 1893, with almost 50 newel designs illustrated in the catalog. The posts and other woodworks were available in pine, oak, ash, walnut, and cherry. Even 100 years ago, a premium was charged for works made of walnut and cherry. Those of imported mahogany commanded an even greater premium.

The newel posts illustrated are of turned designs, octagon designs with stave construction, fancy molded construction, and construction with raised panels. The constructed newels were inlaid or carved.

Stair rails, referred to as handrails today, were designed in thickness proportional to the width. The designs ranged from the simplest to the most complex. The complex designs included curves on curves, curves with side coves, compound curves with base coves, off-center handholds, curves and beads, compound joints of two or more components, &c. Widths ranged from around three inches to over seven inches. Stair rails were considered to be the topping off of a well designed stair structure.

Better homes and business offices built in the 1890s usually included an elegant staircase, at least from the entry floor to the second or third floor, since these were the areas most frequented by visitors. The staircases illustrated in the catalog recognized the demand for such high quality woodwork. The catalog includes layout plans for such staircases and landings, as well as illustrations of newel posts, risers, steps, balusters, and handrails.

Verandas, Porches, and Balustrades

The exterior of a house or office received as much attention in the design detail of the woodworks as the interior. The sides and corners of porches and verandas were accented with turned or chamfered and carved columns. Turned columns included combinations of plinth, torus, ball, bead, cove, astragal, ovolo, cavetto, reed, abacus, &c. Columns tapered from bottom to top and also from top to bottom, depending upon the visual effect to be achieved.

Verandas were designed with their own complement of spindles. Outside balusters, both turned and sawn, are richly illustrated. Combinations of plinth blocks, end turnings, carved brackets, and fretwork were used to fill out the design details for added elegance.

Brackets and Window Hoods

Nearly 100 separate designs of carved, fluted, and raised pattern brackets were offered to the trade and are illustrated in this volume. Brackets were used in interior and exterior designs. Any corner or cove could be enhanced with an appropriately designed bracket. Roof gables, too, could be finished with decorative touches of the millwork, fretwork, and wood rosettes that were offered.

And no window would be complete without a complementary window hood. For interior accents, a complement of cornice drapery and verge boards are illustrated.

Corner, Plinth, and Head Blocks — Wooden Ornaments

A great variety of patterns were manufactured for corner, plinth, and head blocks, all of wood and sold in lots of a hundred. White pine and yellow pine were the wood materials of choice where surfaces were to be painted. Red oak and birch blocks and ornaments were available for a 5% premium and walnut for a 100% premium. The finer hardwoods were seemingly intended for use where clear, unpainted, finishes were to be used. Carved blocks "in endless varieties" were offered "at a small additional cost" over turned blocks. Carved and turned blocks are illustrated throughout the catalog.

Door and window framing, baseboard woodwork, and variety of rails are illustrated. This trim work was used in conjunction with carved ornaments to accent the corners of door facings and window frames. For the tops of both interior and exterior doors, over 75 head block and trim designs were offered.

Hardwood Mantels

The catalog illustrates 22 pages of designs for fireplace mantels. The stock size of mantels was five feet in width. For sizes up to five feet six inches, wall plates were extended. For larger or smaller sizes, a custom order could be placed. The more economical mantels were made of red oak and birch in standard sizes and in large production quantities. Other domestic hardwood was available on order and included cherry, white oak, sycamore, gum, ash, redwood, maple, and butternut. Extra special woods also available for mantels included mahogany, prima vera, bird's-eye maple, curly birch, white wood (yellow poplar), and gold wood (species indeterminable). Gold wood was presumably painted and gilded, though the catalog is unclear on this point.

To complete the fireplace, a variety of enameled and embossed tiles were offered with the colors and tints selected to harmonize best with the wood. Brass and wrought iron goods, including andirons, fire sets, grates, linings, &c. could also be shipped with mantels. The only things not included for the building of an elegant fireplace were "75 common brick and a little mortar" presumably acquired locally.

In reviewing the designs of mantels, take special note of the incorporation of carved blocks and turnings in the designs.

Pulpits and Pew Ends

Several designs are illustrated for pulpits, from the simple to the more elaborate and distinctive. Nine designs of pew ends show the attention to detail associated with the building of meeting houses of the 1893 era.

Interior Hardwood Finish Mouldings

Your attention is also directed to the 22 pages of interior finish moulding designs illustrated in profile. Any design was available in large or small quantities. To assure service to the customer, any sketched design, or that from another's catalog, "would be cheerfully furnished" as if selected from this catalog . . . and at "reasonable" prices.

Interior finishing was available in maple, ash, red oak, white oak, birch, cherry, sycamore, mahogany, and "all other Woods" in the "best style of workmanship."

Wood Ventilators

Near the end of this book, designs for three ventilators are illustrated. These ventilators were made of wood, both fretwork and carved. The illustrations are among the first that have been found for ventilators. During this era, heating systems had begun to advance toward modern forced-air, requiring duct works and ventilator covers.

A Milepost

To leave a lasting impression, the last page of the 1893 Blumer & Kuhn Stair Co. catalog, most fittingly, illustrates a carved and jointed newel. It is an example of true excellence, one that speaks well for this quality firm and makes its catalog a valuable reference and source of inspiration.

William L. Stephenson Jr.
Loveland, Ohio

Blumer & Kuhn Stair Co.

WHOLESALE MANUFACTURERS OF

STAIRS, STAIR RAILING,

Balusters, Newel Posts, Mantels

Pew Ends, Etc.

ALSO

INTERIOR FINISH

Of every description in all kinds of Hard and Soft Woods

Brackets, Corner and Plinth Blocks,

TURNED PORCH AND VERANDA WORK, ETC.

ST. LOUIS, MO.

CHICAGO:
PUBLISHED BY RAND, MCNALLY & COMPANY,
Printers, Engravers, and Electrotypers.
1893.

INDEX.

E. W. BLUMER, President.   HENRY KUHN, Sec'y & Treas.

Office of
Blumer & Kuhn Stair Co.
MANUFACTURERS OF
BALUSTERS, RAILING
NEWEL POSTS,
AND ALL KINDS OF STAIR MATERIAL.
Dock Street and Broadway.

To the Trade.

ST. LOUIS, MO., May 1, 1893.

Dear Sir:

We take great pleasure in presenting you herewith a copy of our new price list, together with designs for Stair Work, Turned Porch and Veranda Work, Brackets, Corner and Plinth Blocks, Mantels, Church Pews, Mouldings of any design, and especially do we ask you to examine our latest designs for Stair Newel Posts as designated on page 14.

In order to meet the large and increasing demand for our specialties, we were compelled to increase our facilities by the addition of a large and modern Branch Factory, with all the latest and most approved machinery adapted to the different parts of the work. These additional facilities together with the Parent Factory, will enable us to meet all demands made upon us promptly and in a more satisfactory manner, both to ourselves and our clients than heretofore.

Our stock on hand is at all times large and of the choicest grades, being thoroughly air-dried, which, with our ample facilities for kiln-drying, enables us to furnish work that we can guarantee to be satisfactory, being executed by competent and skilled workmen, of which we employ only the best.

We shall be pleased to receive your orders for anything in our line, and will cheerfully quote you prices on memoranda or details for any of the above class of work.

Inviting a personal inspection of our stock, and hoping to receive your orders, we are

Yours truly,

Blumer & Kuhn Stair Co.

STAIR PLANS.

Stairs, Newel Posts
✳ Balusters
Stair Railing.

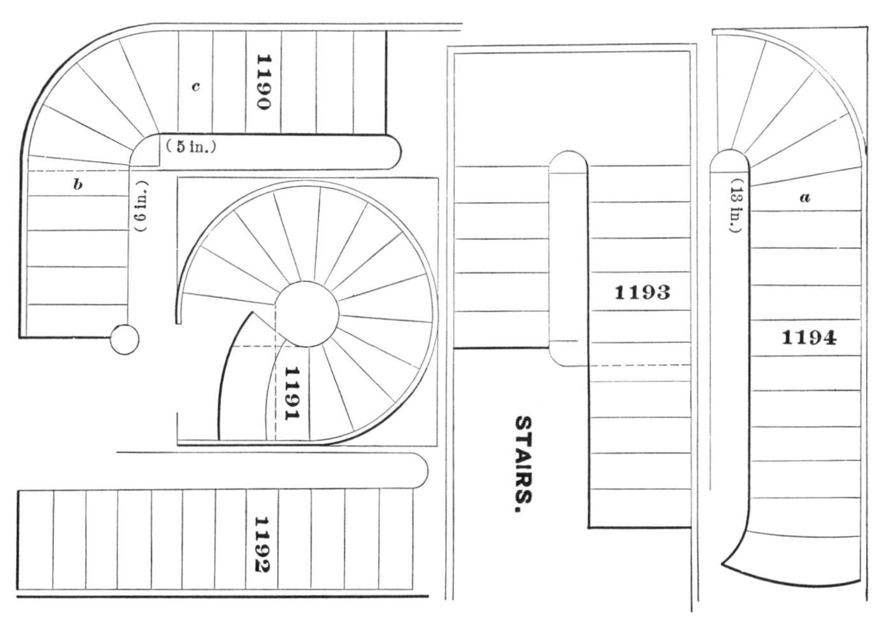

STAIRS, NEWEL POSTS, BALUSTERS, STAIR RAILING, ETC.

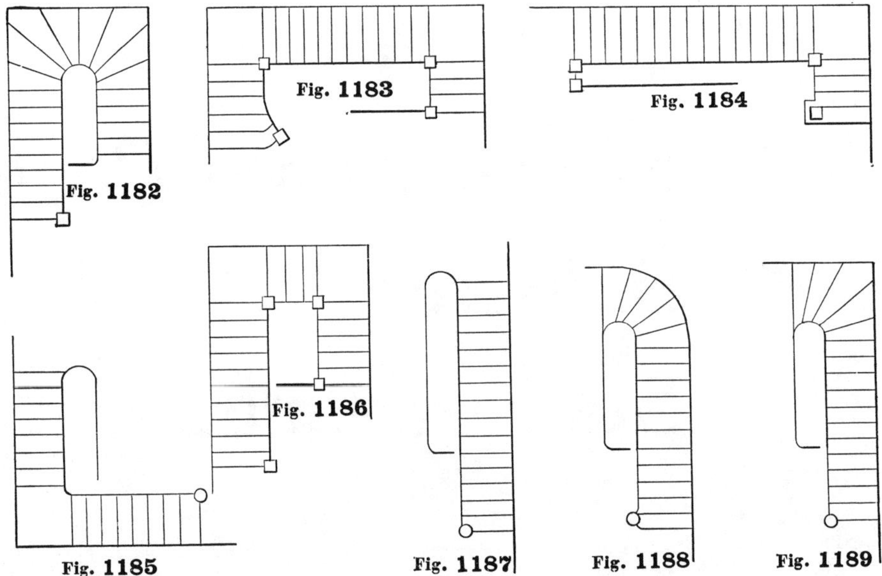

Fig. 1182   Fig. 1183   Fig. 1184

Fig. 1185   Fig. 1186   Fig. 1187   Fig. 1188   Fig. 1189

DIRECTIONS NECESSARY FOR ORDERING STAIRS AND STAIR RAILING.

When a flight of stairs is wanted, we should know the height of story from floor to floor, width of joists in second story, width and run of stairs, the size of cylinder, style of base used in the hall, with rough sketch showing about the shape of stairs wanted.

FOR STAIR RAILING, STRAIGHT FLIGHT,

We require the width of rise and step as sawed out on string board, the number of risers, the size of cylinder from face to face of string or face board, which way it turns at head of stairs, and the number of feet of straight rail required at landing. Unless we receive plan showing otherwise, we always suppose the top riser for a straight flight of stairs to be placed at the edge or spring of cylinder.

FOR CIRCULAR OR WINDING STAIRS,

We should have an exact plan of stairs as built, giving the width of rise and step, the location of risers in cylinder, etc.; and, when there are straight steps below or above the cylinder, always give the distance from the first square riser to the edge or spring line of cylinder, on the face of string or face board. *Always write your address in full on the plans.*

PRICE LIST OF STAIR WORK.

LIBERAL DISCOUNT TO DEALERS.

BALUSTERS.

We turn all our Stair Balusters 2 ft. 4 in. and 2 ft. 8 in. long, unless otherwise ordered. Are prepared to furnish, on short notice, any length or style desired. Odd lengths cost extra.

Fancy Turned Balusters.

Nos. 1200 and 1201.

Sizes.	1½ in.	1¾ in.	2 in.	2¼ in.	2½ in.
	Cts.	Cts.	Cts.	Cts.	Cts.
Oak or Ash...	9	12	12	15	17
Wal't or Ch'ry,	11	17	17	21	23

Nos. 1202 and 1203.

Sizes.	1½ in.	1¾ in.	2 in.	2¼ in.	2½ in.
	Cts.	Cts.	Cts.	Cts.	Cts.
Oak or Ash....	11	14	14	17	19
Wal't or Ch'ry.	13	19	19	23	25

Nos. 1206 to 1214 inclusive.

Sizes.	1¾ in.	2 in.	2¼ in.	2½ in.	2¾ in.
	Cts.	Cts.	Cts.	Cts.	Cts.
Oak or Ash....	17	17	20	22	30
Wal't or Ch'ry.	22	22	26	28	43

Octagon Balusters.

No. 1205.

Sizes.	1¾ in.	2 in.	2¼ in.	2½ in.	2¾ in.
	Cts.	Cts.	Cts.	Cts.	Cts.
Oak or Ash....	19	19	23	25	35
Wal't or Ch'ry.	24	24	29	31	48

For No. 1204, Fluted, add to list of No. 1205 1c. Mahogany costs about double price.

NEWELS.

Fancy Turned Newel Posts.

Nos. 1300 and 1301.

Sizes.	4 in.	5 in.	6 in.	7 in.
Pine....................	$ .90	$1.25	$1.50	
Oak or Ash.............	3.00	3 50	4.00	$4.50
Walnut or Cherry......	3.50	4.00	4.50	5.00

Plain Octagon Staved Newel Posts.

No. 1302, Walnut, Cherry, Oak, or Ash.

Sizes.	8 in.	9 in.	10 in.	11 in.	12 in.
Prices.	$5.75	$6.00	$6.25	$6.50	$7.00

For Raised O G Panels, add to above prices $1.50 each.

For Mahogany Posts, add to above prices $4.00 each.

Octagon Sunk Panel Newel Posts.

FANCY MOULDED.

No. 1303, Walnut, Cherry, Oak, or Ash.

Sizes.	8 in.	9 in.	10 in.	11 in.	12 in.
Prices.	$8.50	$9.00	$9.50	$10.00	$10.50

For Circle Top Panels, add $1.25
For Posts like No. 1304, add $3.00
For Posts like No. 1305, add $4.50

PLATFORM OR ANGLE NEWELS.

Sizes.	Oak or Ash.	Walnut or Cherry.
No. 1501, 5 inch..........	$4.50	$5.00
No. 1502, 5 inch..........	5.00	5.50
No. 1503, 5 inch..........	6.50	7.00
No. 1504, 5 inch..........	5.00	5.50
No. 1505, 5 inch..........	6.50	7.00
No. 1506, 5 inch..........	7.00	7.50

POSTS FOR OUTSIDE BALUSTRADE.

Pine, ordinary lengths (see page 44).

Numbers.	Price, 3¾ inches.	Price, 4¾ inches.	Price, 5¾ inches.
1630	$ .75	$1.00	$1.25
1631	.75	1 00	1.25
1632	1.00	1.25	1.50
1634	1.50	1.75	2.00
1635		1.75	2.00
1639	2.00	2.25	2.50
1640	1.00	1.25	1.50

TURNED BALUSTERS.

For Outside Balustrade see pages 45 and 49.

Prices in Pine or Whitewood.

Length. inches.	8	10	12	14	16	18	20	22	24
	Cts.	Cts.	Cts.	Cts.	Cts.	Cts.	Cts.	Cts.	Cts.
Size, 1¾ x 1¾ in.	6	6	6	7	8	9	11		
Size, 2¾ x 2¾ in.		8	9	10	11	12	13		
Size, 3¾ x 3¾ in.		12	13	14	15	16	17	19	21

SAWED PINE BALUSTERS.

For any of the Patterns on pages 49 and 50, size 5¾ x ⅞ 18 or 20 inches long, price 16 cents each.

PORCH AND VERANDA COLUMNS.

Basswood or Whitewood.

4¾ to 5¾ inches square (pages 45 and 46).

Numbers.	Price, 8 ft. long.	Price, 10 ft. long.
1645	$3.00	$3.50
1646	3.00	3.50
1647	3.00	3.50
1648	3.00	3 75
1648½	4 50	5.50
1649	3.00	3 50
1650	3.00	3.50
1651	3.00	3.50
1652	3.00	3.50
1653	3.00	3.50
1654	3.00	3.50

Discounts to Dealers.

BALUSTERS.

1200
1201
1202
1203
1204
1205
1206
1207
1208
FOR PRICES SEE PAGE 9.
1209
1210
1211
1212
1213
1214

BALUSTERS.

1215
1216
1217
1218
1219
1220
1221
SEND FOR ESTIMATES.
1222
1223
1224
1225
1226
1227

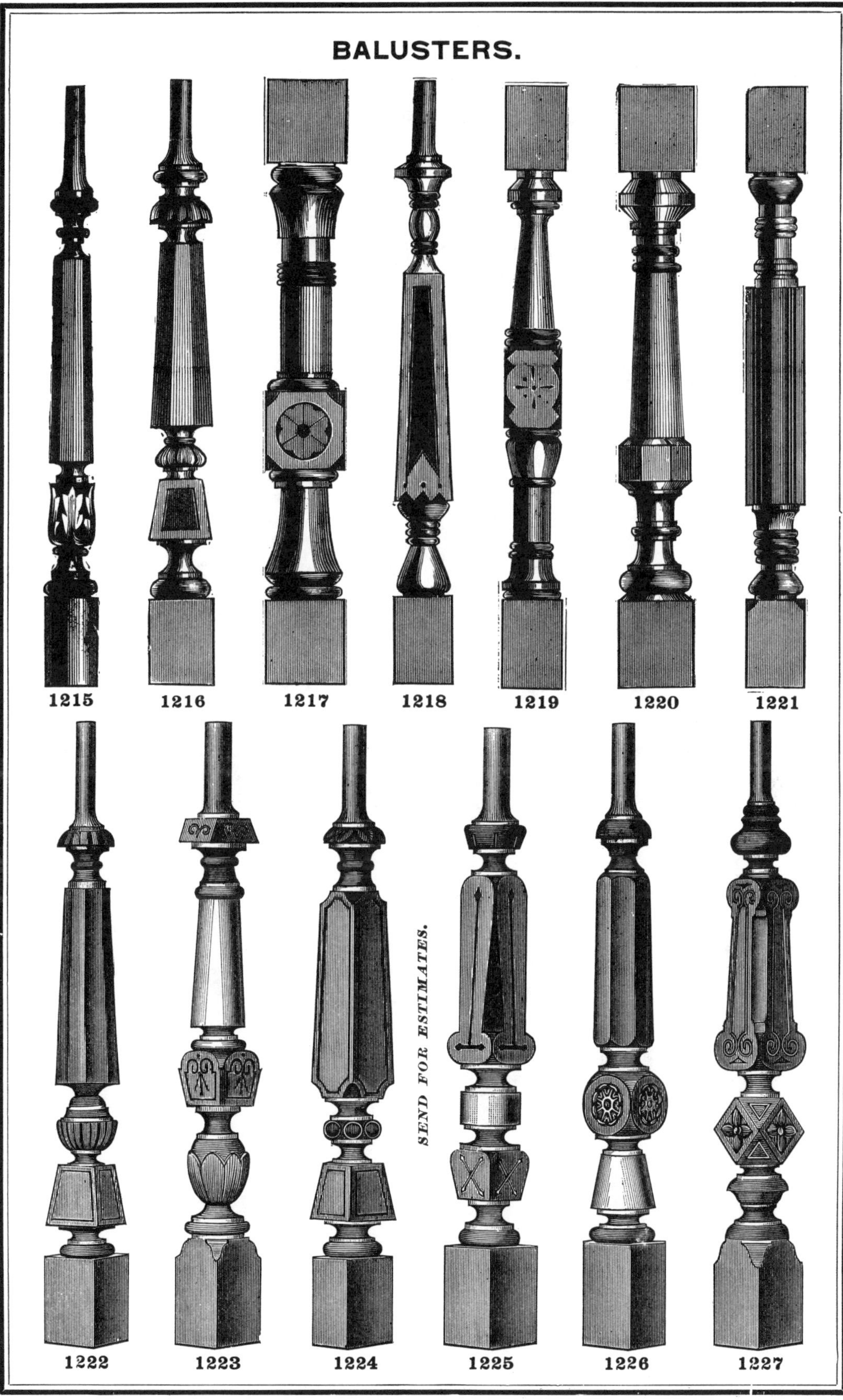

TWISTED BALUSTERS.

WRITE FOR PRICES.

TWISTED BALUSTERS.

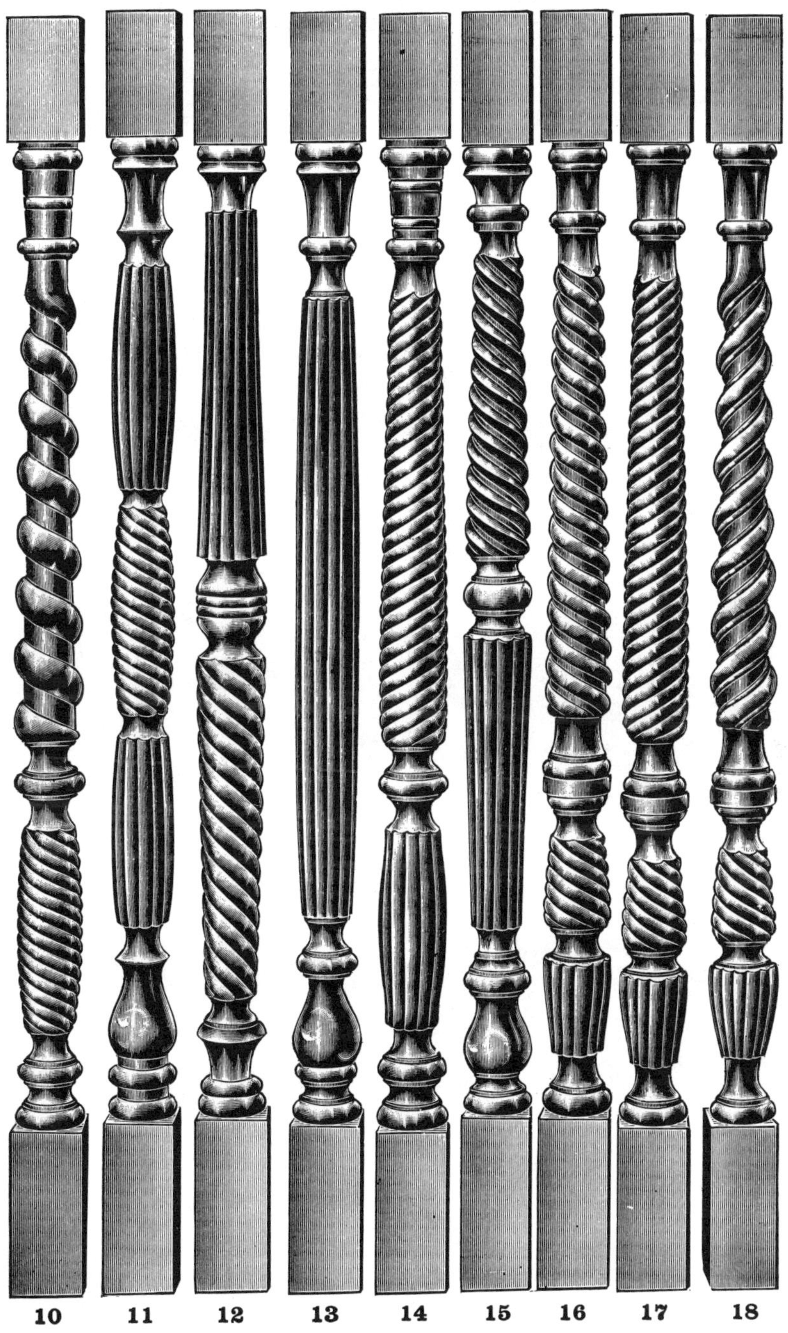

WRITE FOR PRICES.

NEWELS.

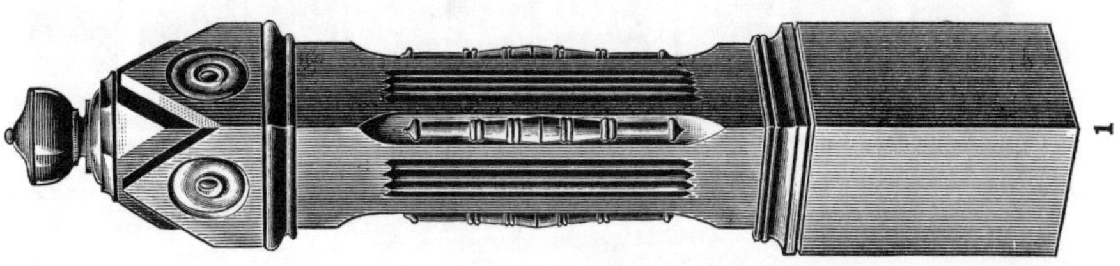

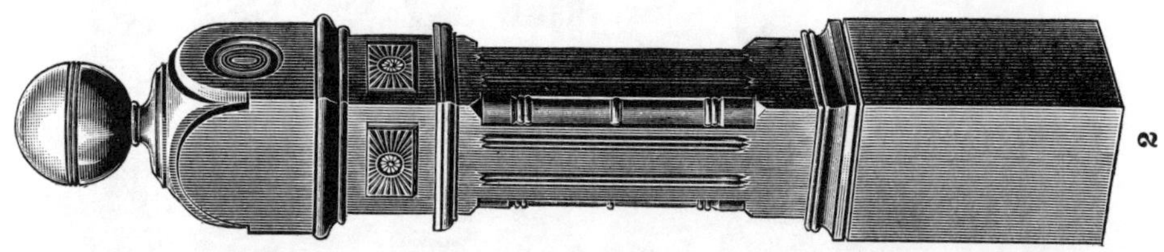

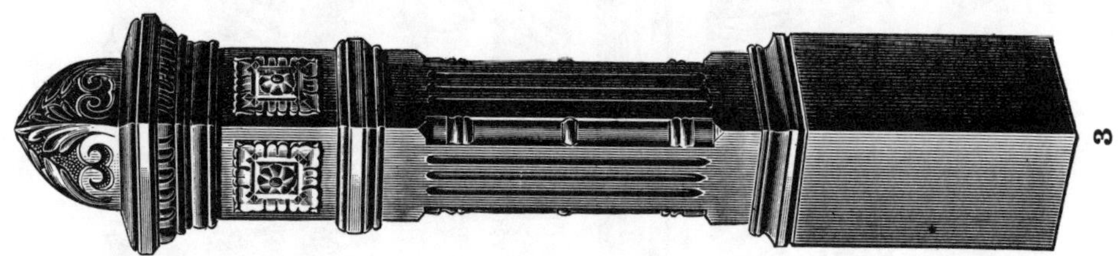

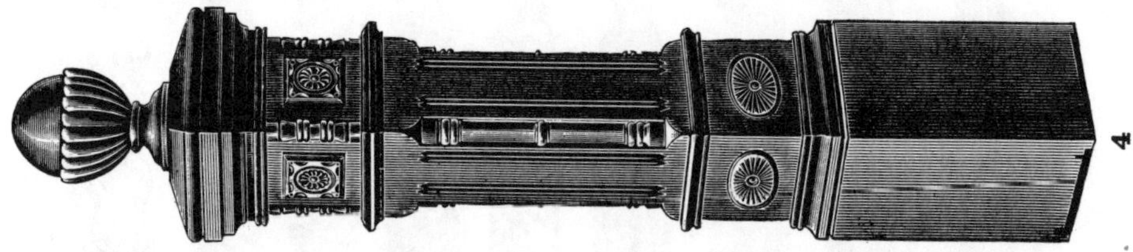

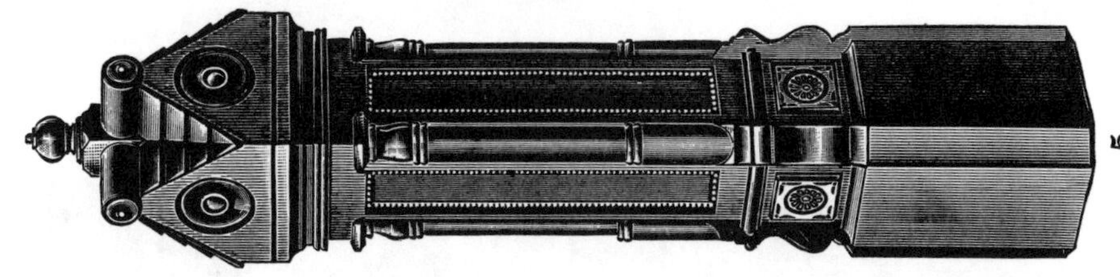

WRITE FOR PRICES.

NEWEL POSTS.

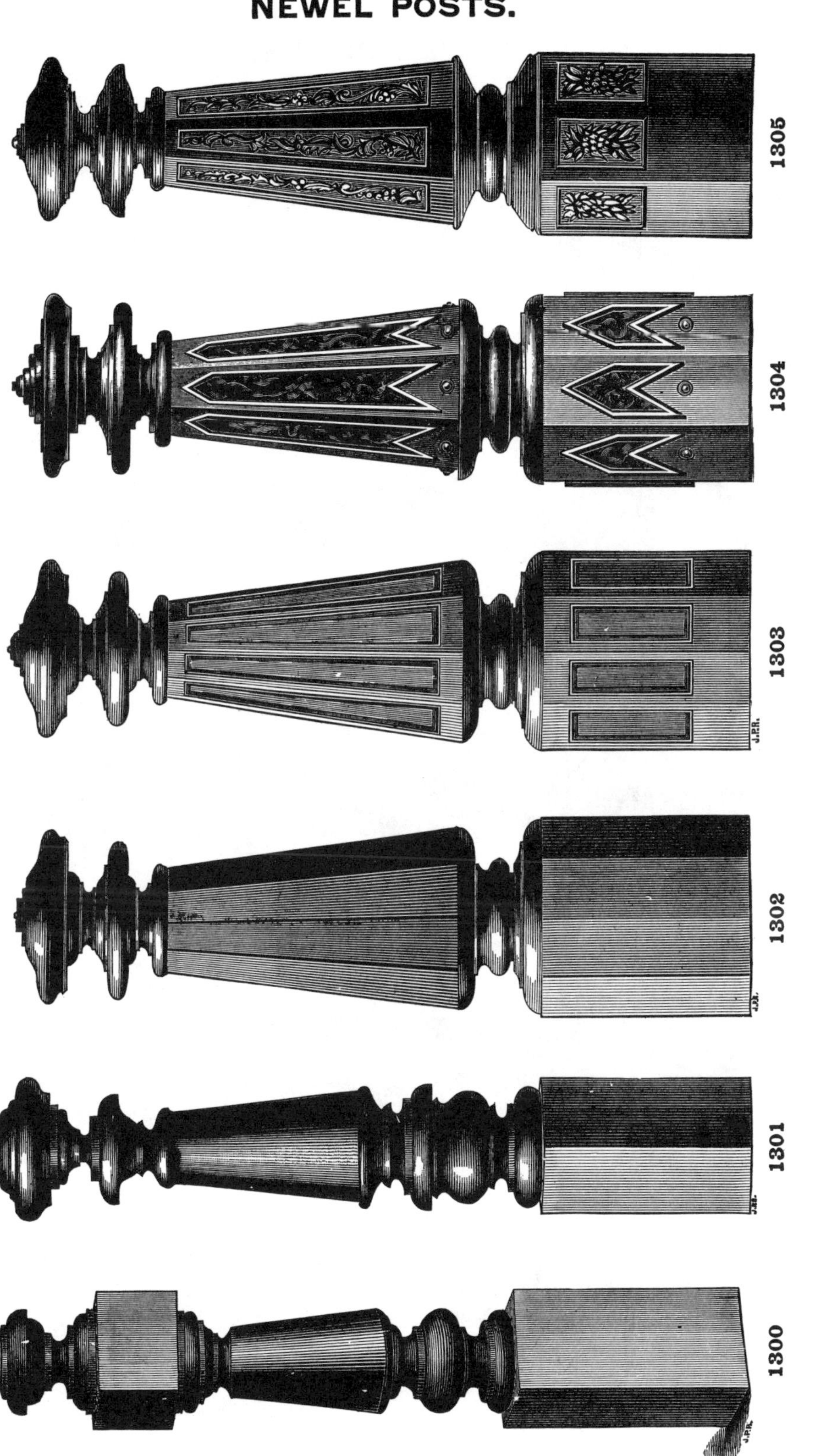

FOR PRICES SEE PAGE 9.

NEWEL POSTS.

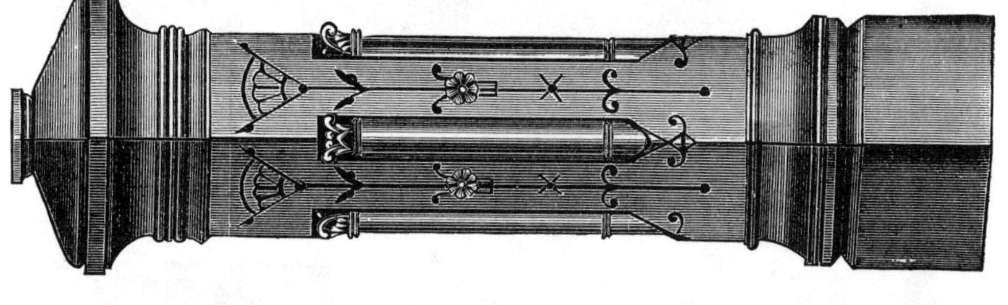

1310

1309

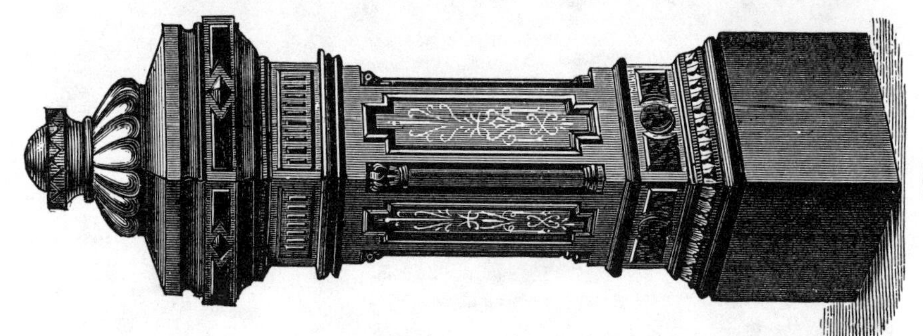

1308

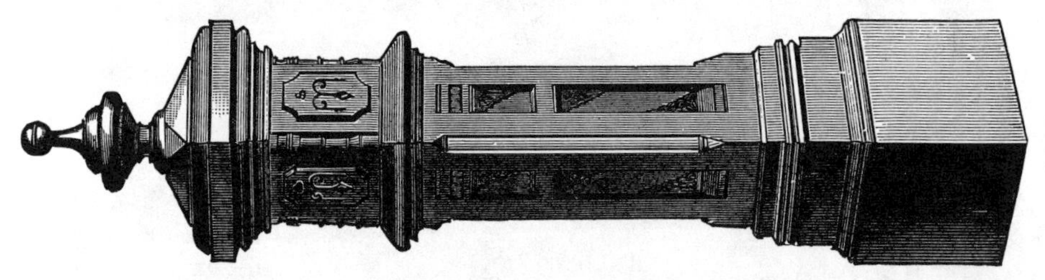

1307

1306

SEND FOR ESTIMATES.

NEWEL POSTS.

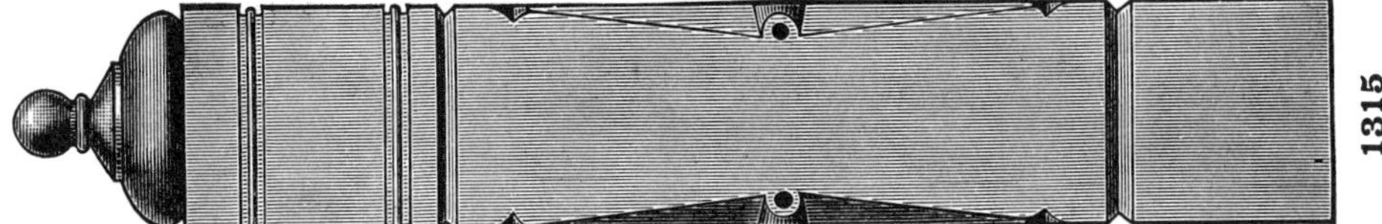

1315

1314

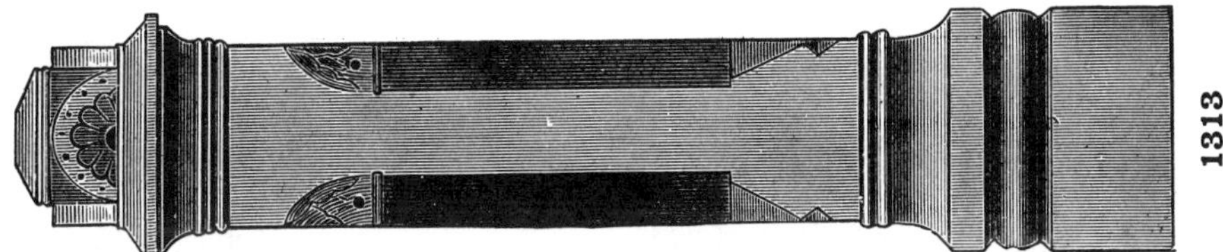

1313

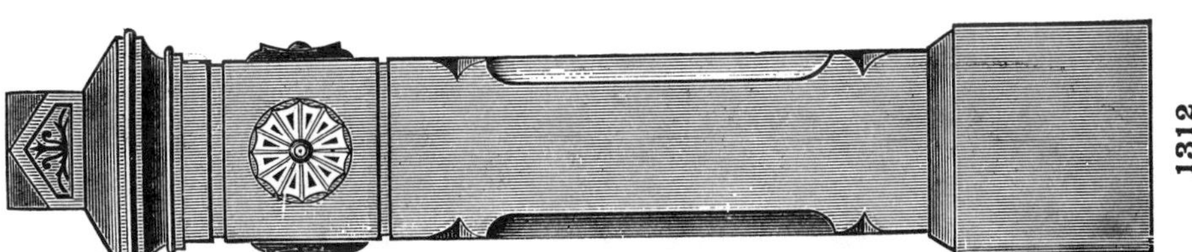

1312

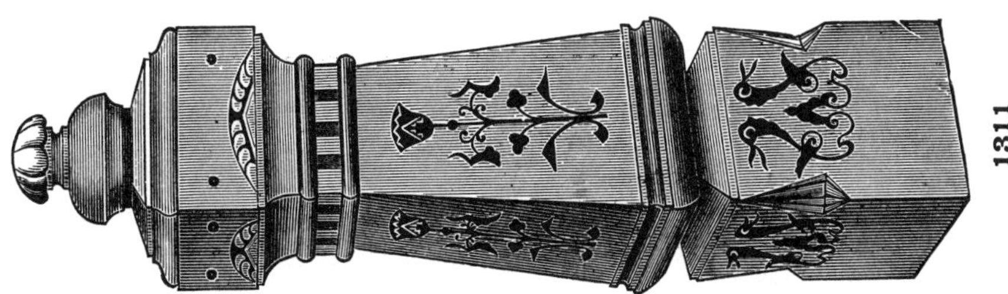

1311

SEND FOR ESTIMATES.

NEWEL POSTS.

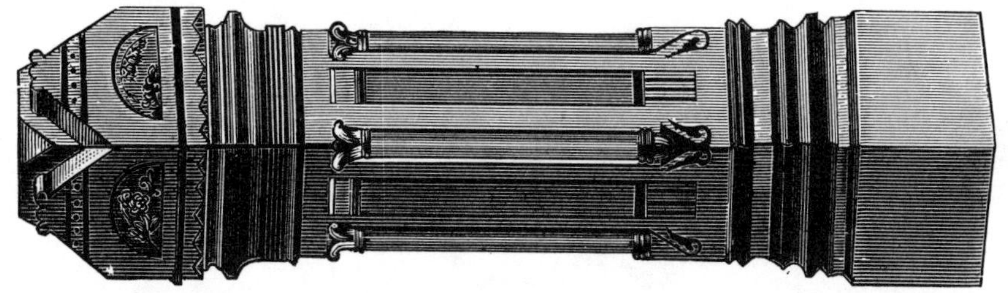

1320

1319

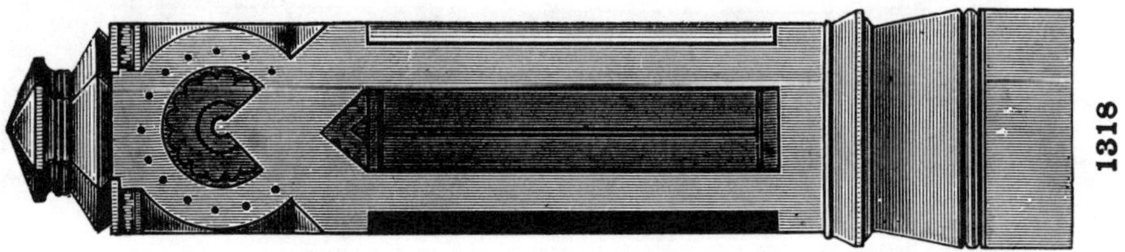

1318

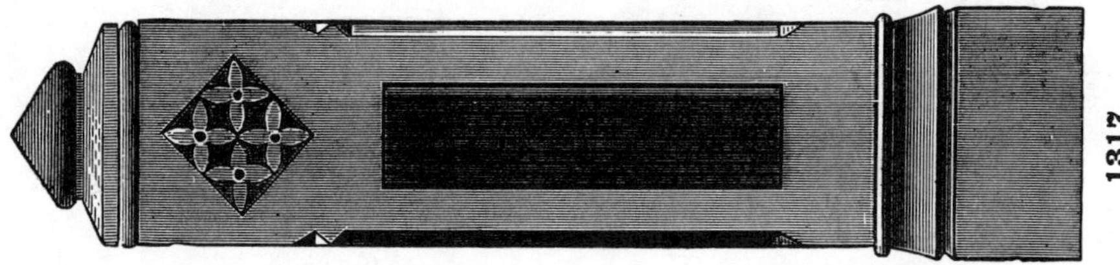

1317

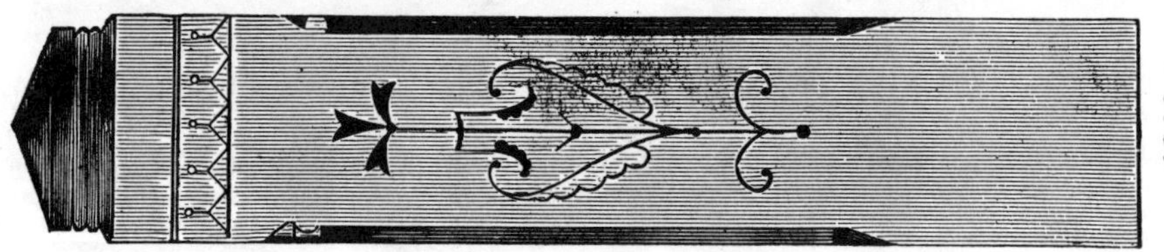

1316

SEND FOR ESTIMATES.

NEWEL POSTS.

1371

1370

1344

1340

1336

1335

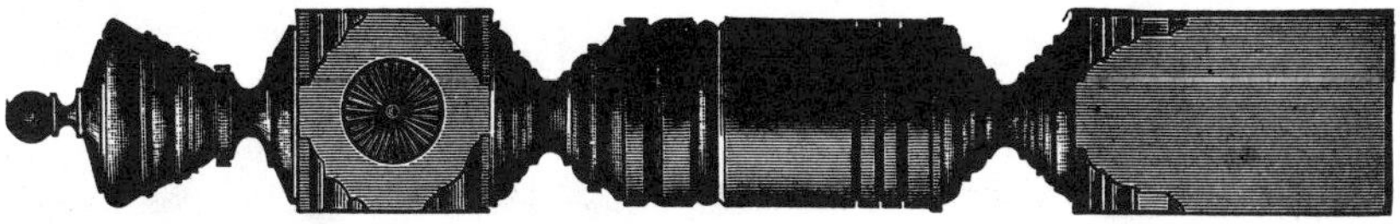

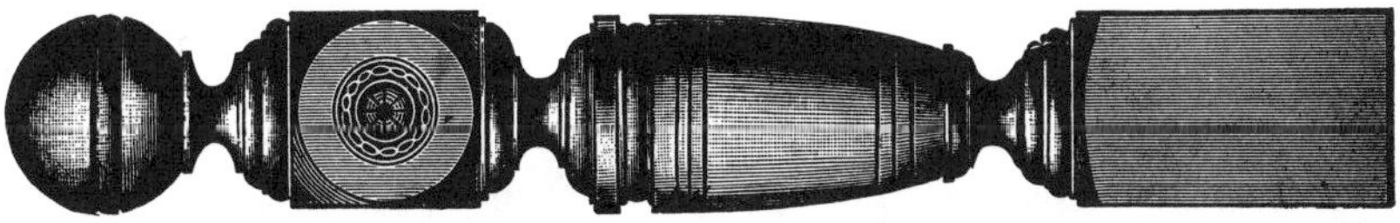

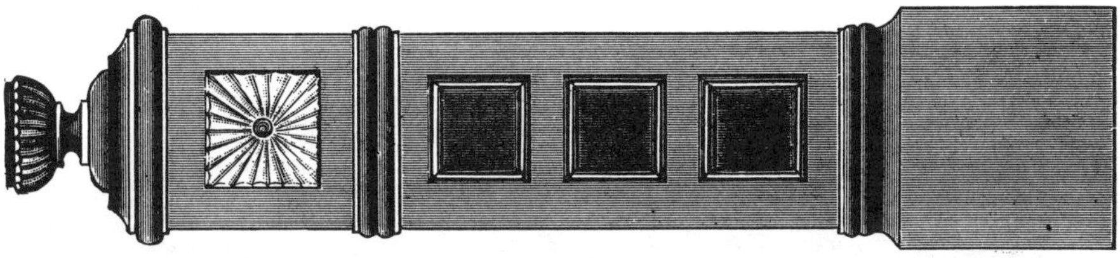

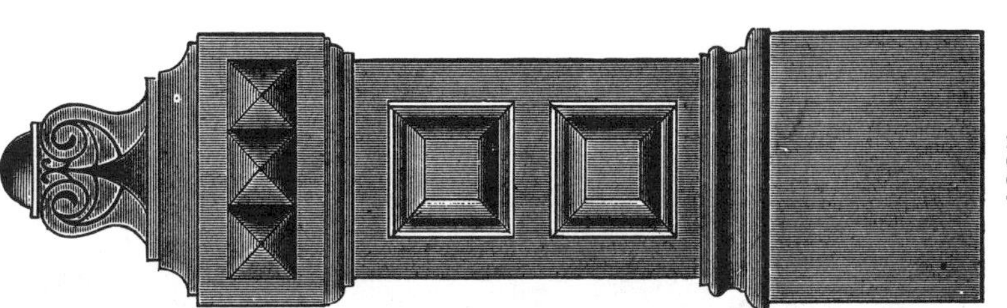

SEND FOR ESTIMATES.

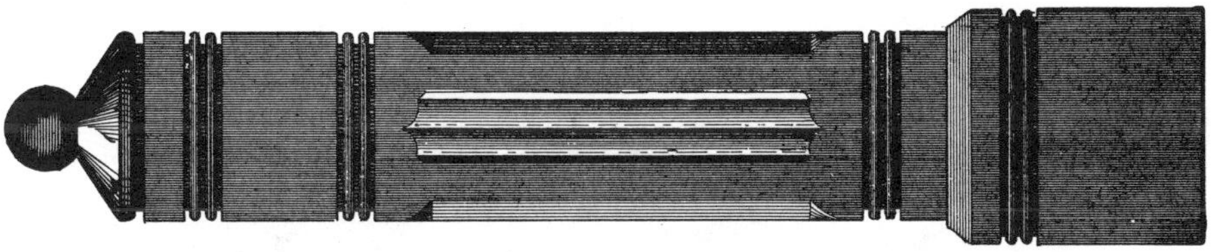

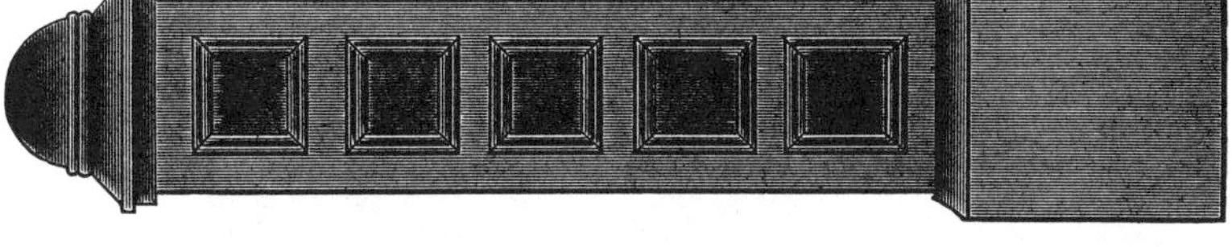

NEWELS.

1331

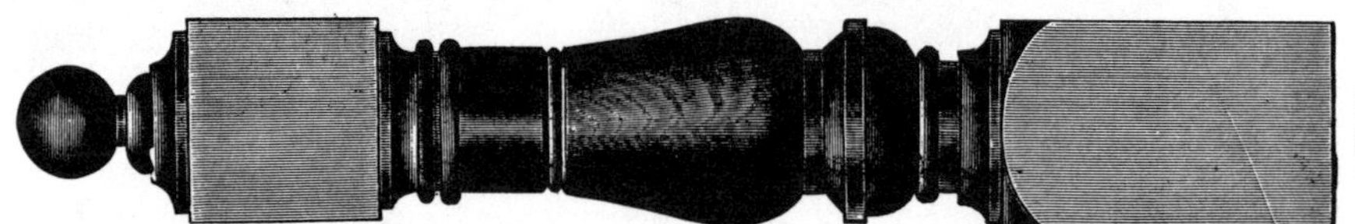

1330

1329

1328

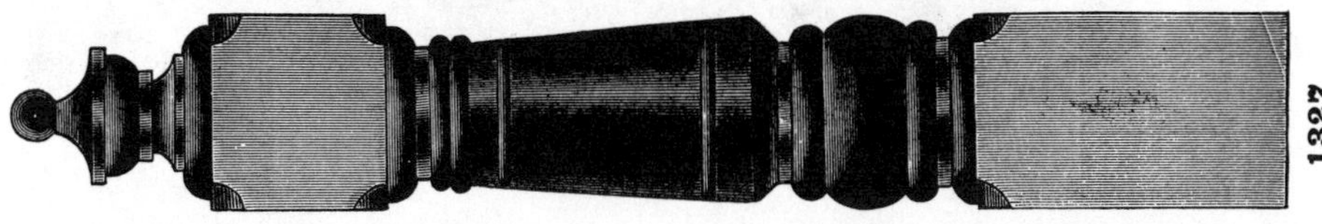

1327

1326

WRITE FOR PRICES.

NEWELS.

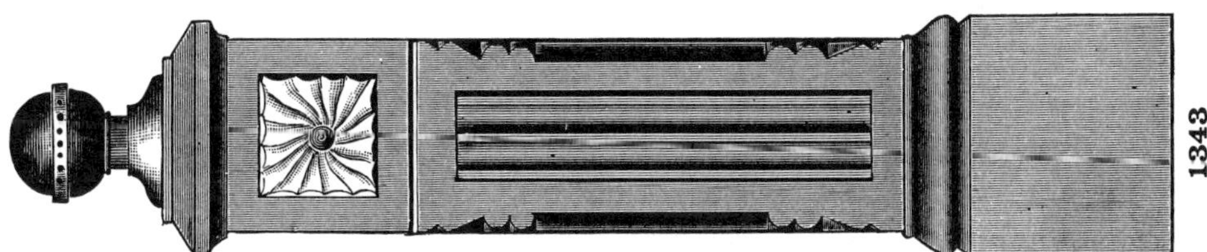

1343

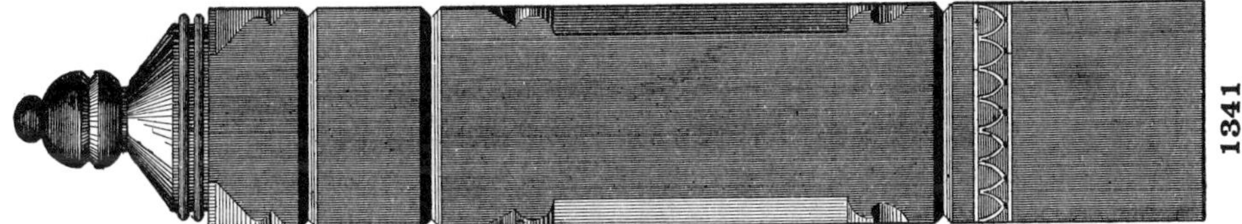

1341

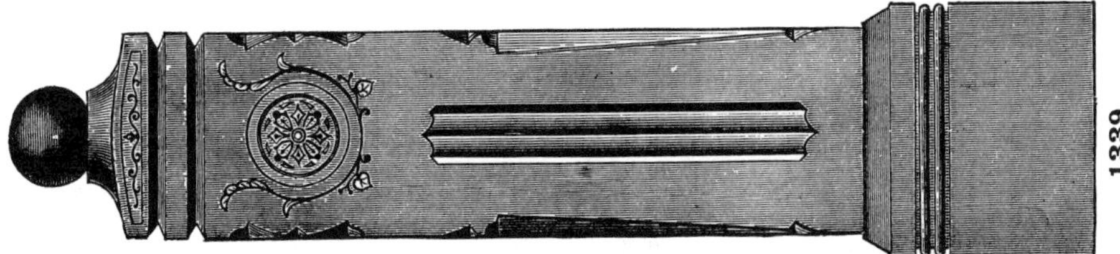

1339

WRITE FOR PRICES.

STAIR RAILS.

Thickness of Rails varies from 1¾ to 2¾, proportionate to width.

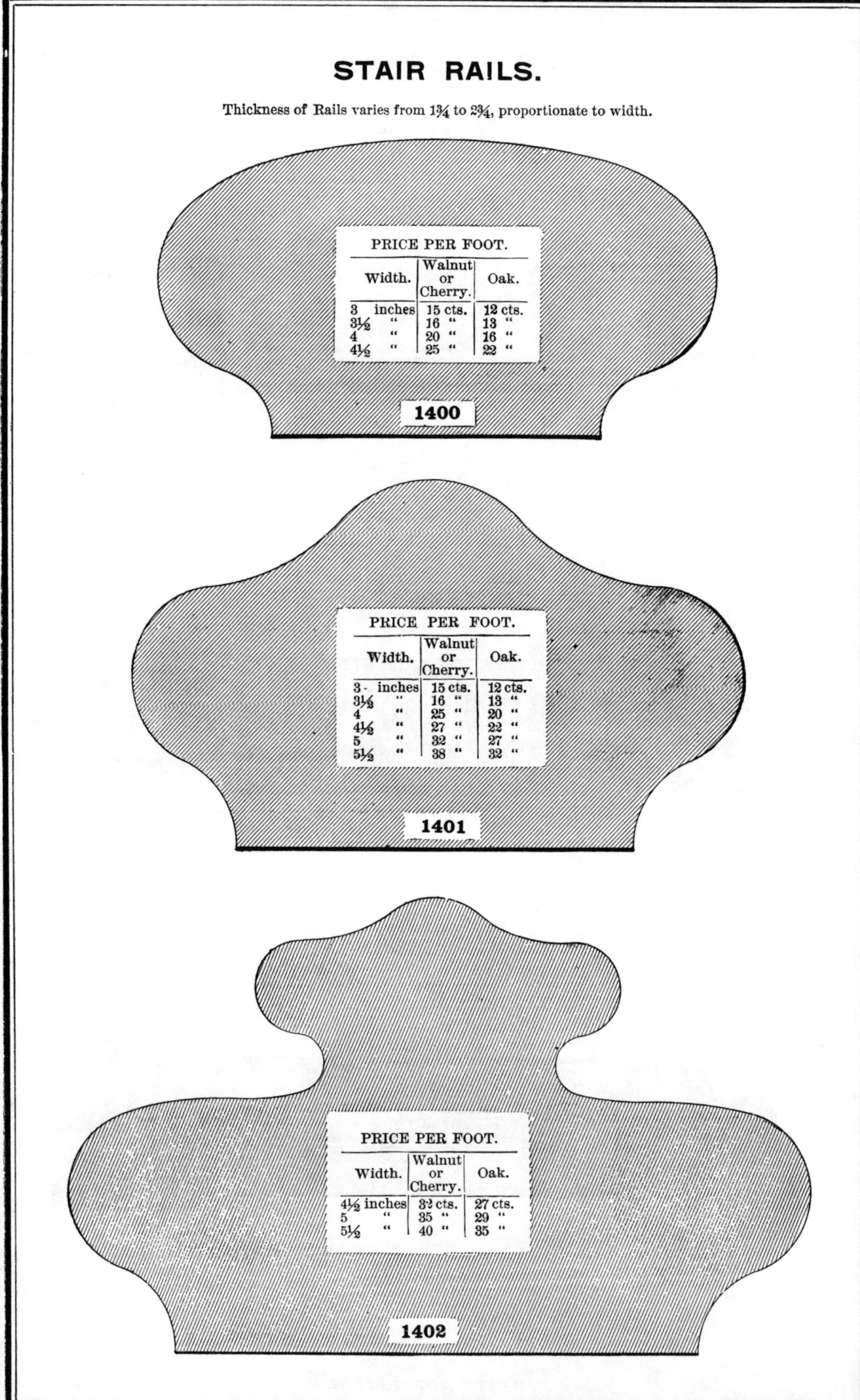

PRICE PER FOOT.

Width.	Walnut or Cherry.	Oak.
3 inches	15 cts.	12 cts.
3½ "	16 "	13 "
4 "	20 "	16 "
4½ "	25 "	22 "

1400

PRICE PER FOOT.

Width.	Walnut or Cherry.	Oak.
3 - inches	15 cts.	12 cts.
3½ "	16 "	13 "
4 "	25 "	20 "
4½ "	27 "	22 "
5 "	32 "	27 "
5½ "	38 "	32 "

1401

PRICE PER FOOT.

Width.	Walnut or Cherry.	Oak.
4½ inches	32 cts.	27 cts.
5 "	35 "	29 "
5½ "	40 "	35 "

1402

STAIR RAILS.

Thickness of Rails varies from 1¾ to 2¾, proportionate to width.

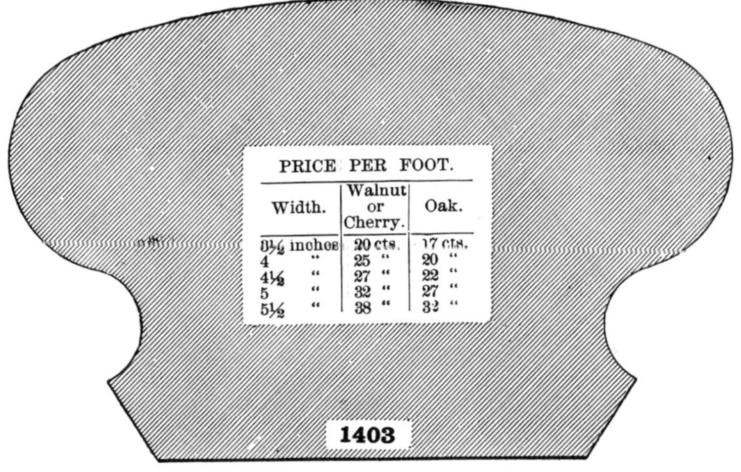

PRICE PER FOOT.		
Width.	Walnut or Cherry.	Oak.
3½ inches	20 cts.	17 cts.
4 "	25 "	20 "
4½ "	27 "	22 "
5 "	32 "	27 "
5½ "	38 "	32 "

1403

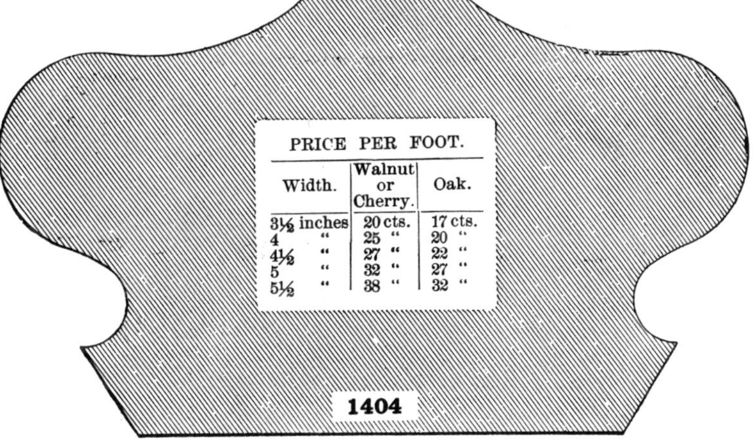

PRICE PER FOOT.		
Width.	Walnut or Cherry.	Oak.
3½ inches	20 cts.	17 cts.
4 "	25 "	20 "
4½ "	27 "	22 "
5 "	32 "	27 "
5½ "	38 "	32 "

1404

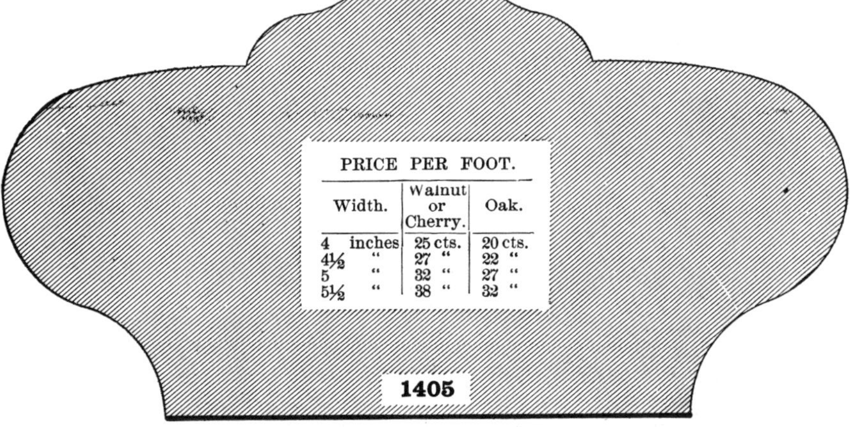

PRICE PER FOOT.		
Width.	Walnut or Cherry.	Oak.
4 inches	25 cts.	20 cts.
4½ "	27 "	22 "
5 "	32 "	27 "
5½ "	38 "	32 "

1405

STAIR RAILS.

Thickness of Rails varies from 1¾ to 2¾, proportionate to width.

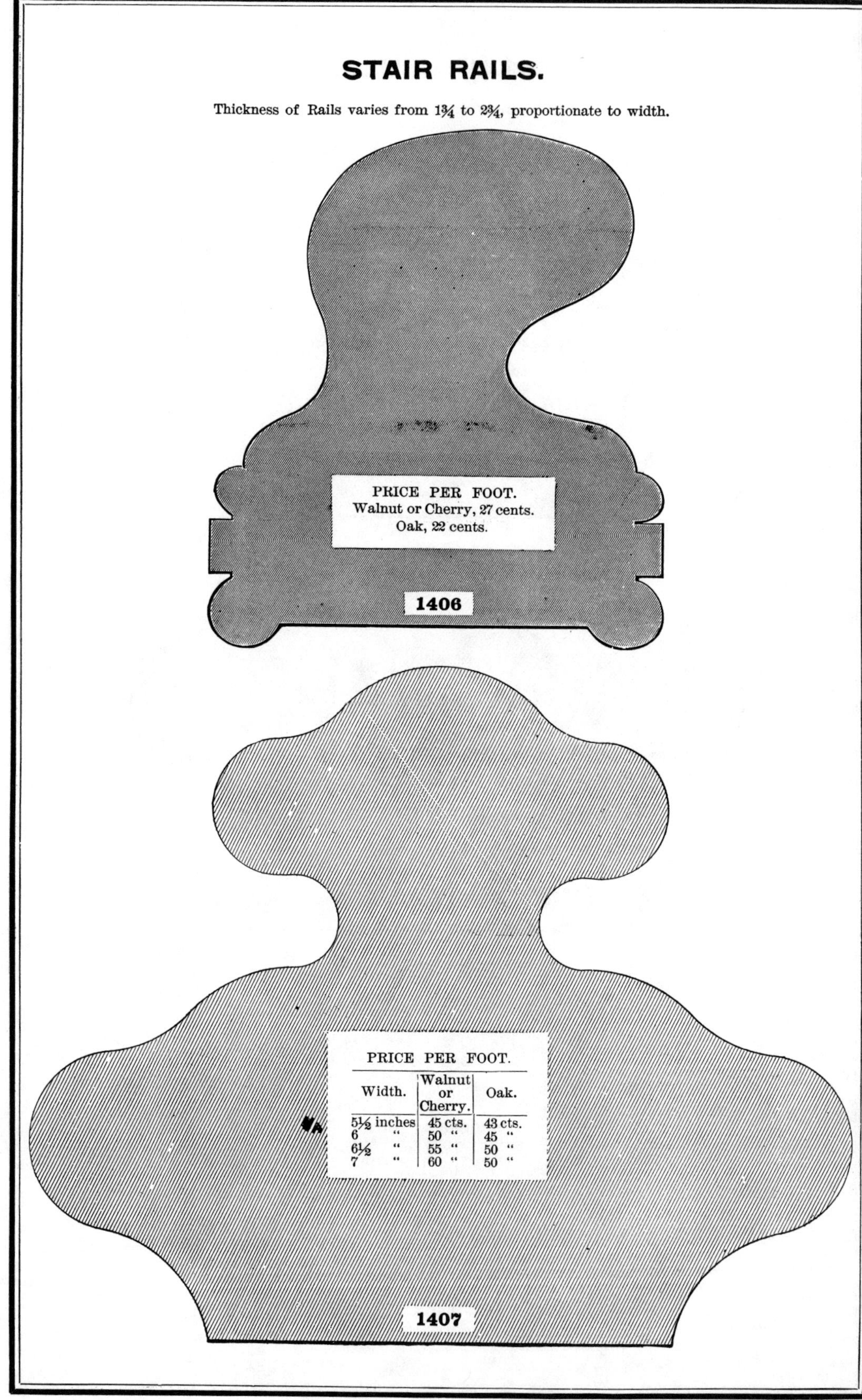

PRICE PER FOOT.

Width.	Walnut or Cherry.	Oak.
5½ inches	45 cts.	43 cts.
6 "	50 "	45 "
6½ "	55 "	50 "
7 "	60 "	50 "

STAIR RAILS.

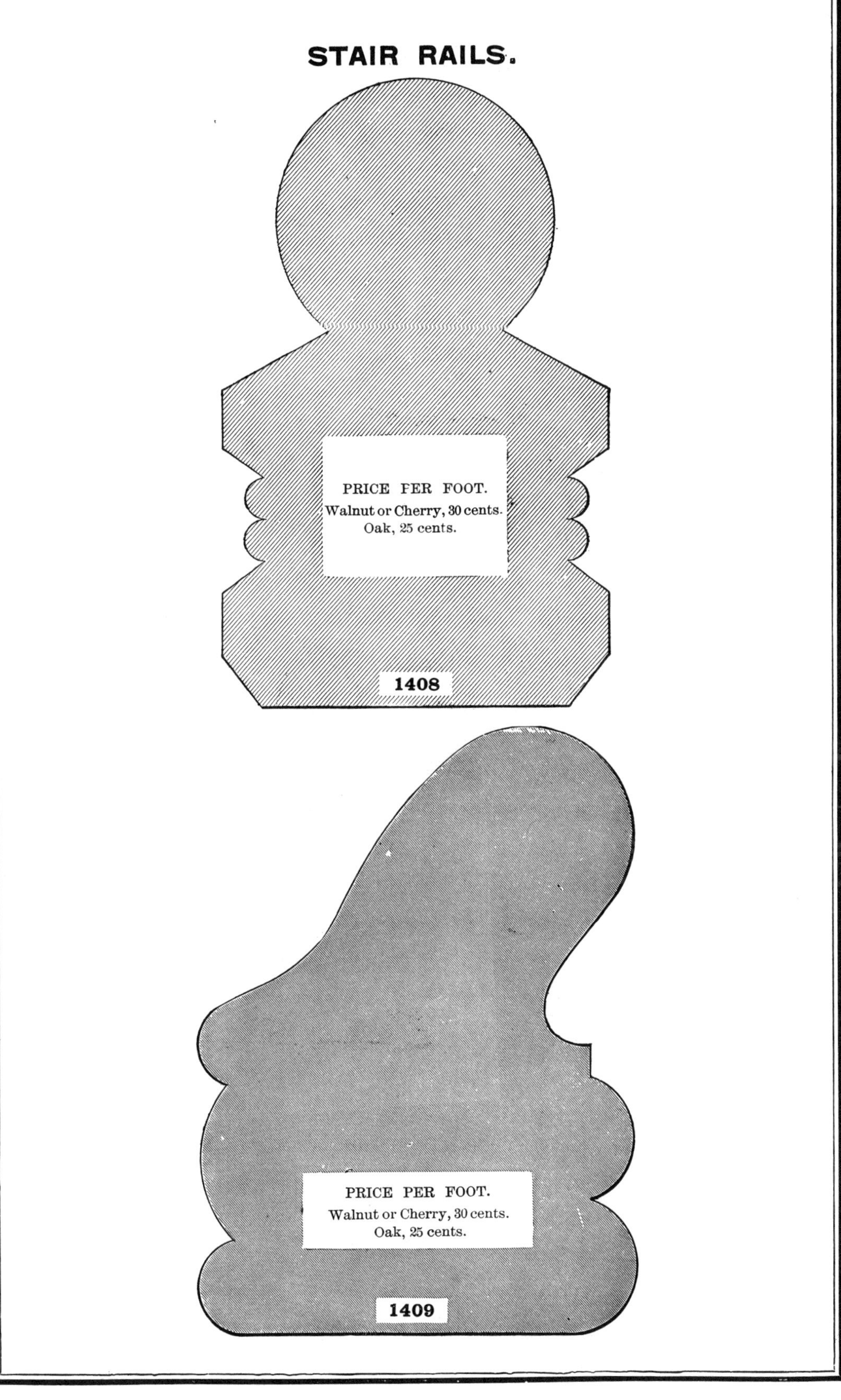

STAIR RAILS.

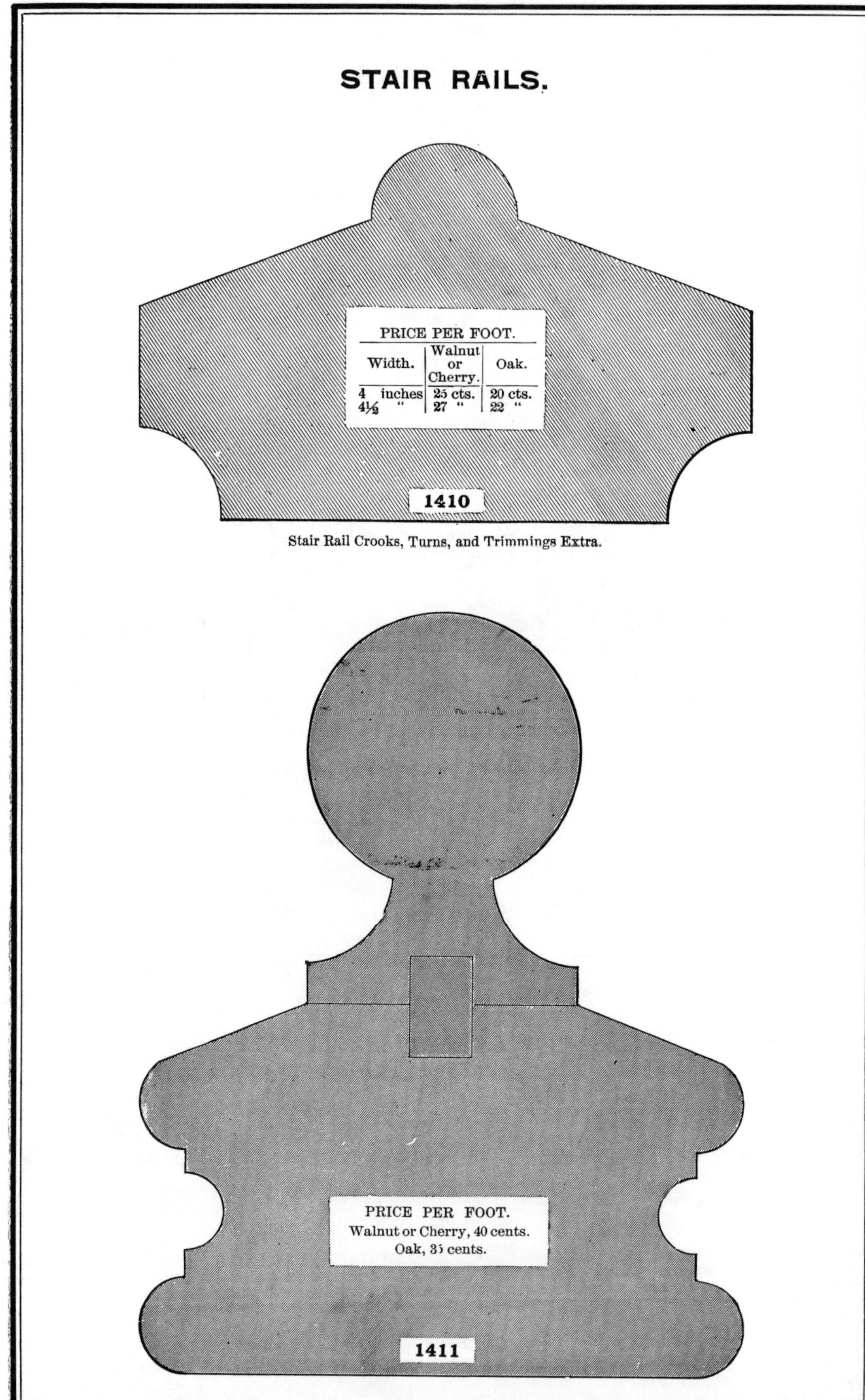

Width.	Walnut or Cherry.	Oak.
4 inches	25 cts.	20 cts.
4½ "	27 "	22 "

1410

Stair Rail Crooks, Turns, and Trimmings Extra.

PRICE PER FOOT.
Walnut or Cherry, 40 cents.
Oak, 35 cents.

1411

STAIR RAILS.

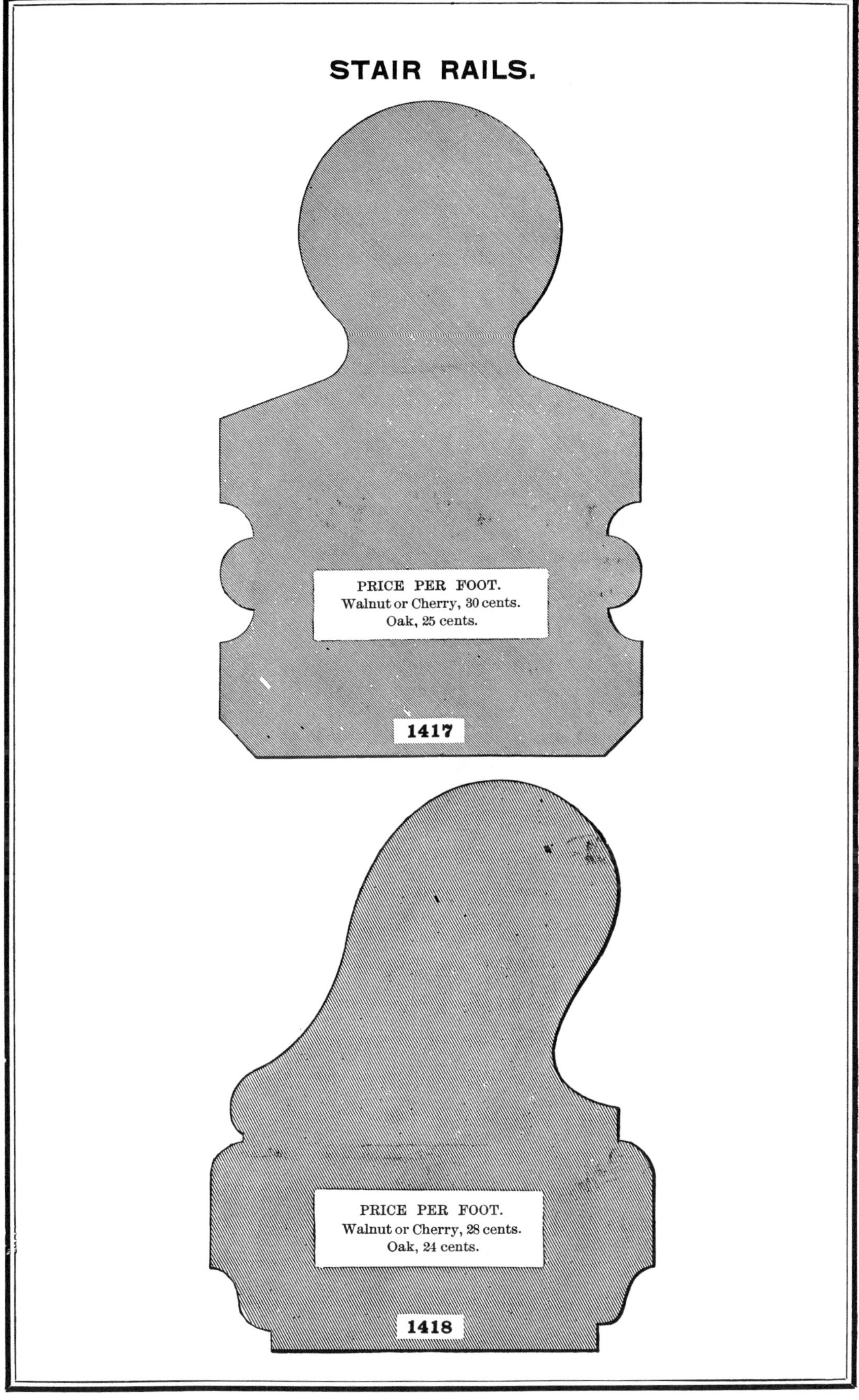

STAIR RAILS.

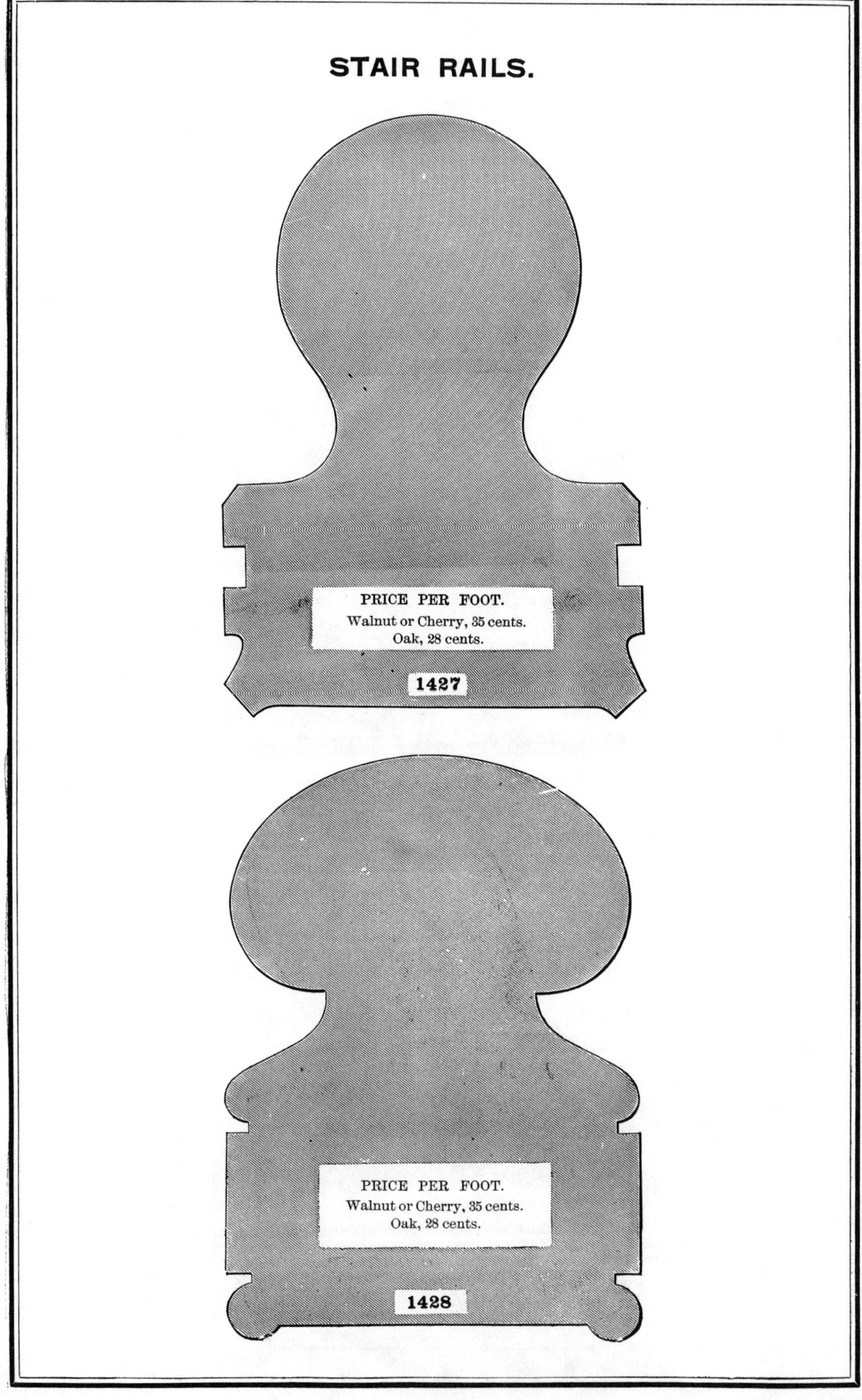

PLATFORM NEWELS.

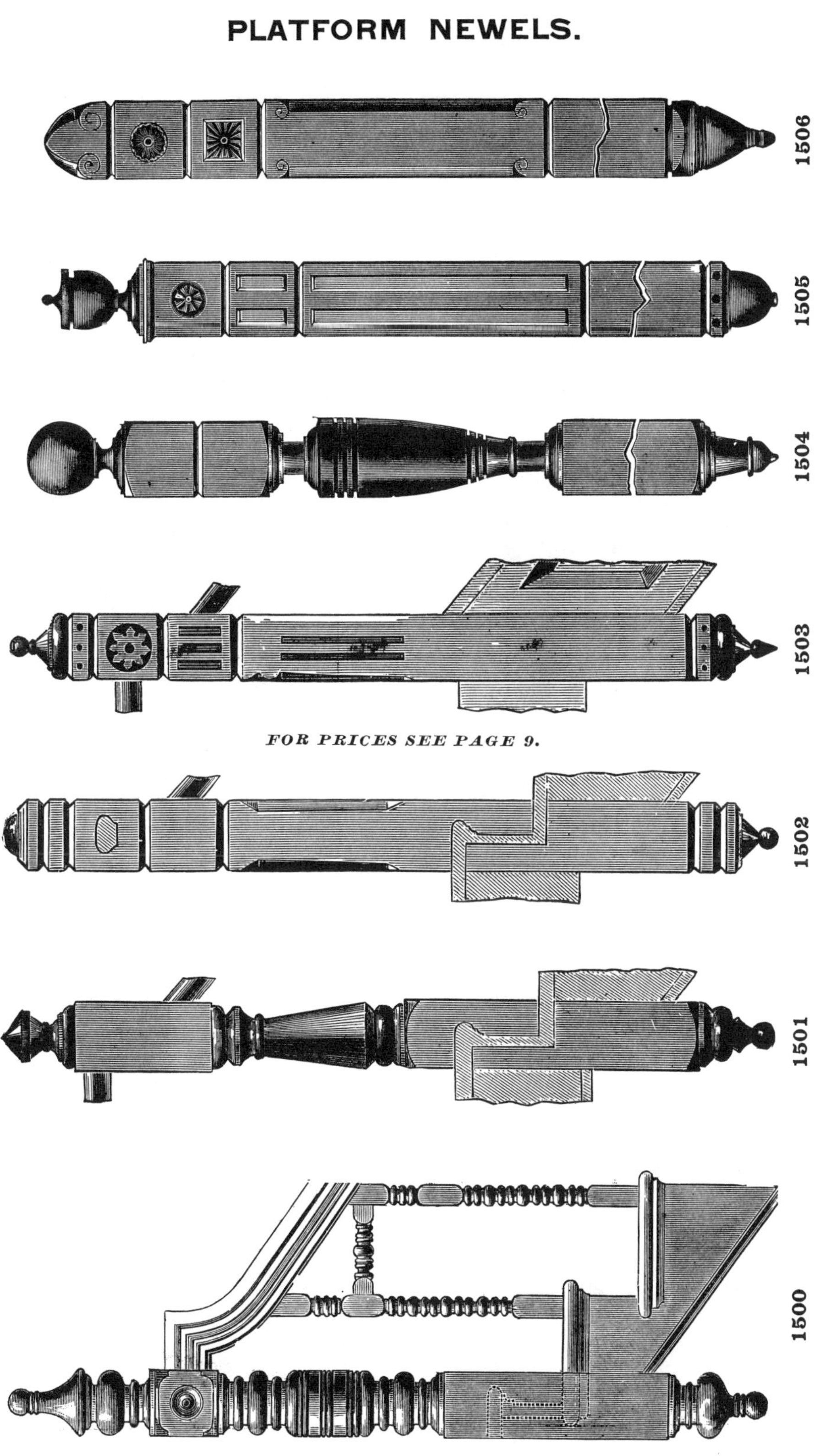

FOR PRICES SEE PAGE 9.

DESIGNS FOR STAIRS.

1520

1521

1522

1523

WRITE FOR PRICES.

DESIGNS FOR STAIRS.

1524

1525

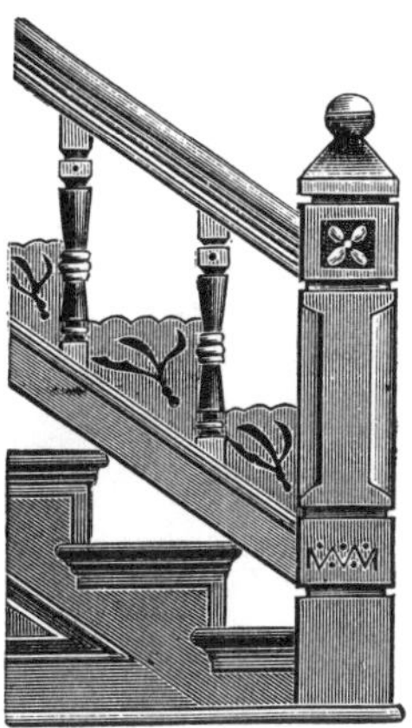

1526

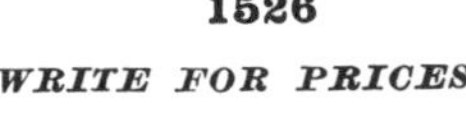

1527

WRITE FOR PRICES.

DESIGN FOR STAIRS.

1528

DESIGN FOR STAIRS.

WRITE FOR PRICES.

1529

DESIGN FOR STAIRS.

1530

DESIGN FOR STAIRS.

1531

WRITE FOR PRICES.

DESIGN FOR STAIRS.

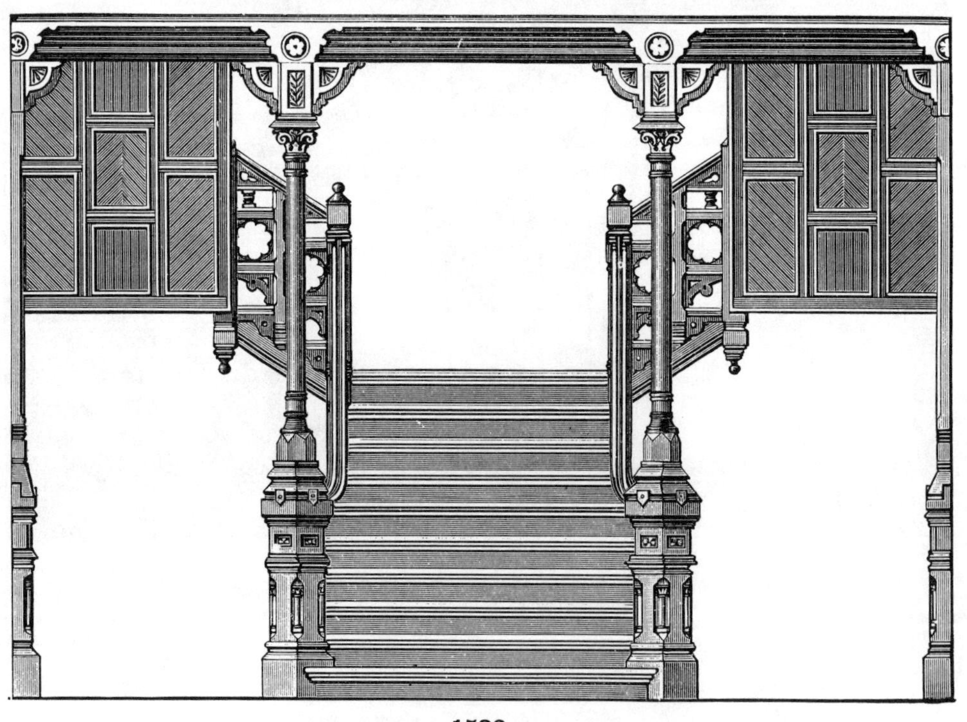

1532

WRITE FOR PRICES.

DESIGNS FOR STAIRS.

1533

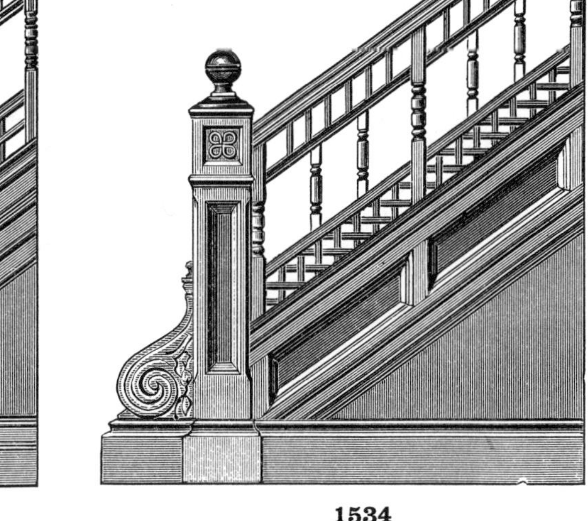

1534

1535

1536

WRITE FOR PRICES.

DESIGNS FOR STAIRS.

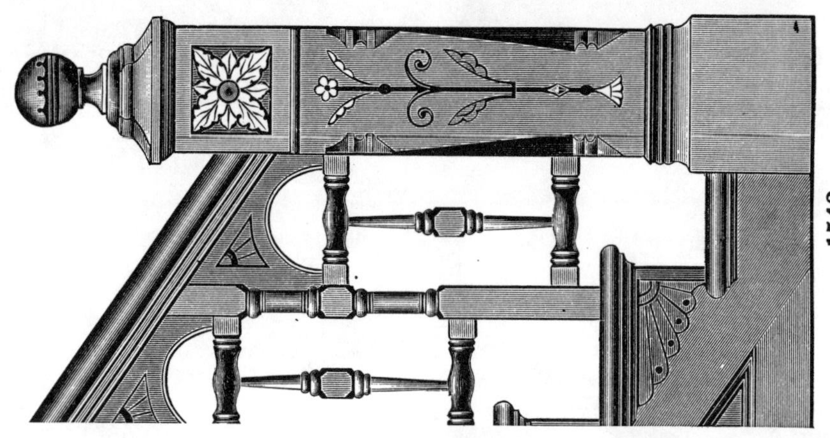

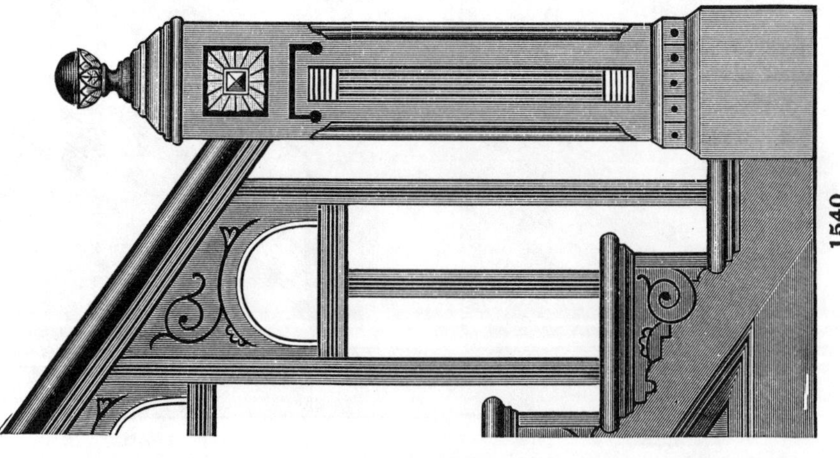

WRITE FOR PRICES.

DESIGNS FOR STAIRS.

1551

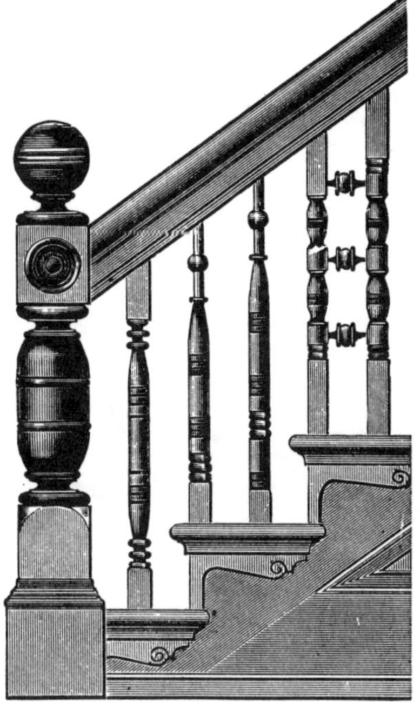

1552

1553

1554

WRITE FOR PRICES.

PORTIERE WORK.

675

Made any Size.

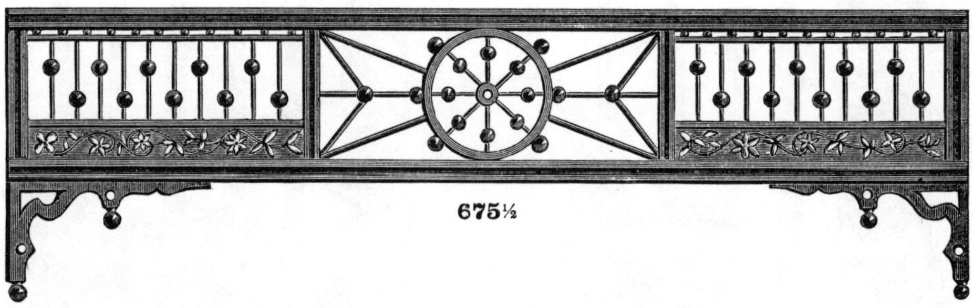

675½

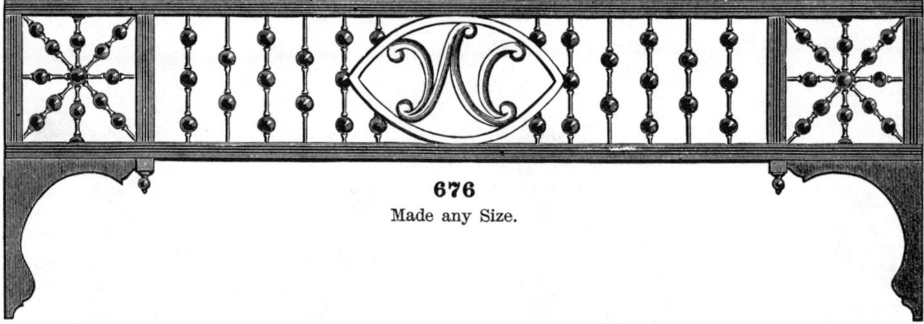

676

Made any Size.

678

Portière Work of all Descriptions Made to Order.

WRITE FOR PRICES.

STAIR BRACKETS.

Level Brackets for Stairs, 4 inches wide. ¼ inch thick.   Price per foot: Pine, 6 cents; Black Walnut, 10 cents.

Stair Brackets, 8 to 10 inches long. Walnut, 10 cents; Pine, 6 cents each;

OUTSIDE RAILS.

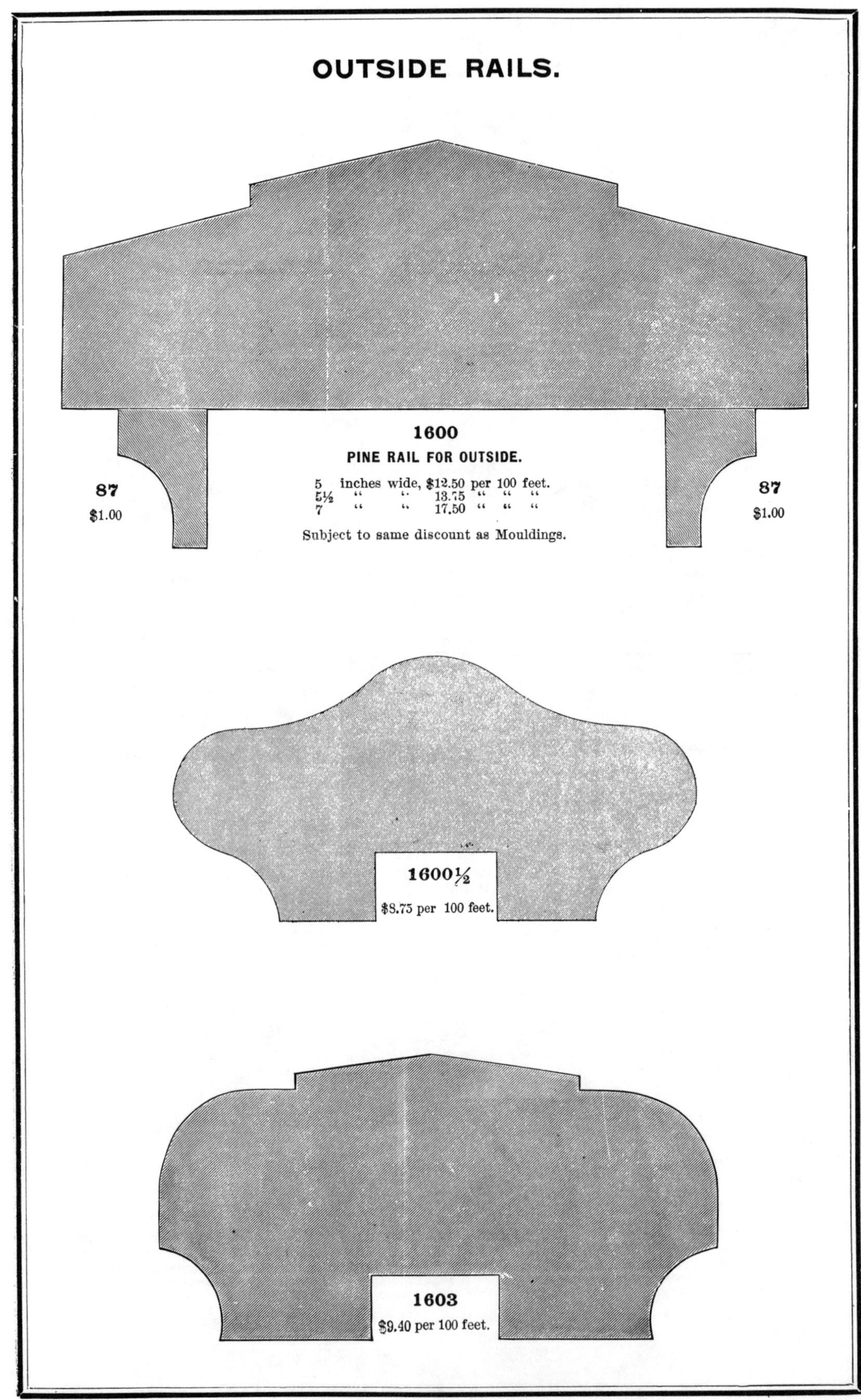

RAILS AND BASE FOR OUTSIDE.

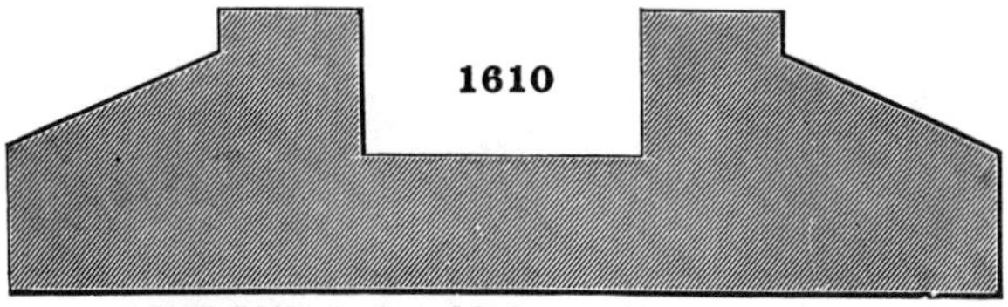

1610

FOOT RAIL, for Sawed Balusters, $8 00 per 100 feet.

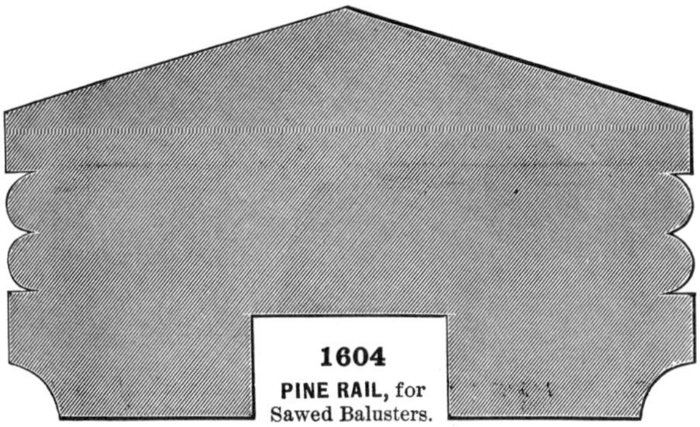

1604
PINE RAIL, for
Sawed Balusters.
$7.50 per 100 feet.   Subject to discount.

1611

$9 40 per 100 feet.

1606
PINE RAIL, FOR PORCHES.
$9.25 per 100 feet.   Subject to discount.   Used also for Base by
omitting the Half-Round, for which deduct $1.75 per 100.

1612 $9.40 per 100 feet.

NEWELS FOR BALUSTRADE AND PORCH WORK.

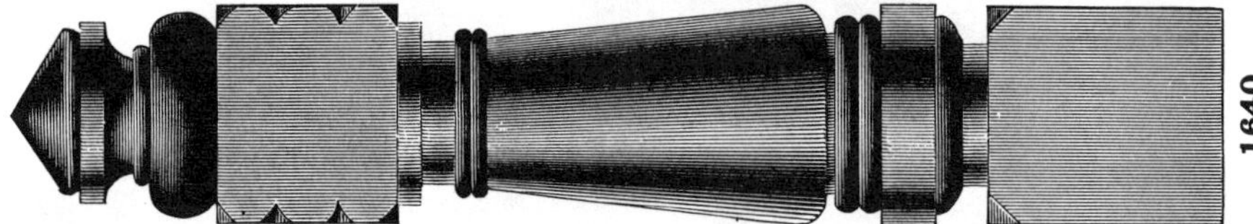

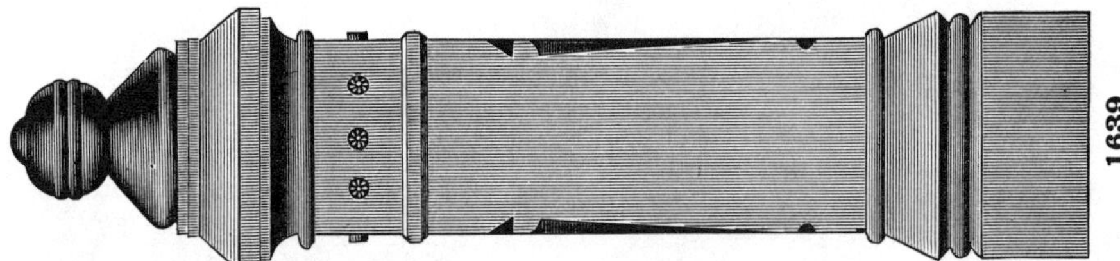

FOR PRICES SEE PAGE 9.

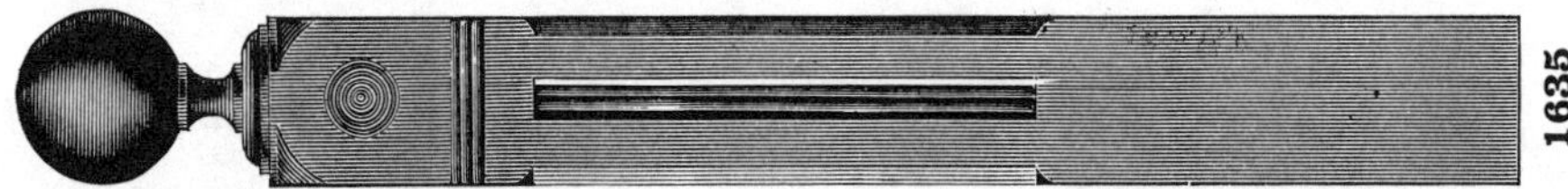

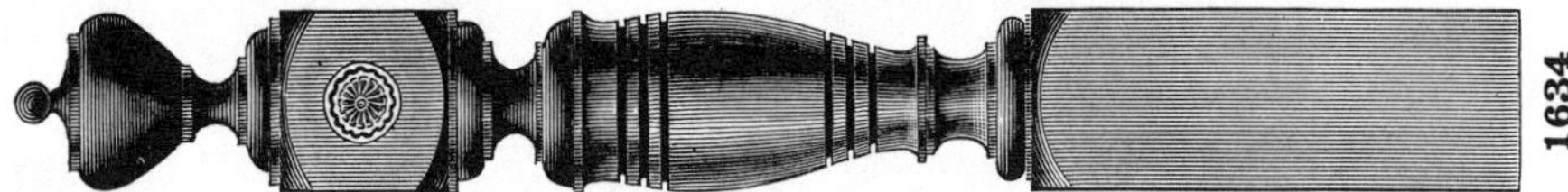

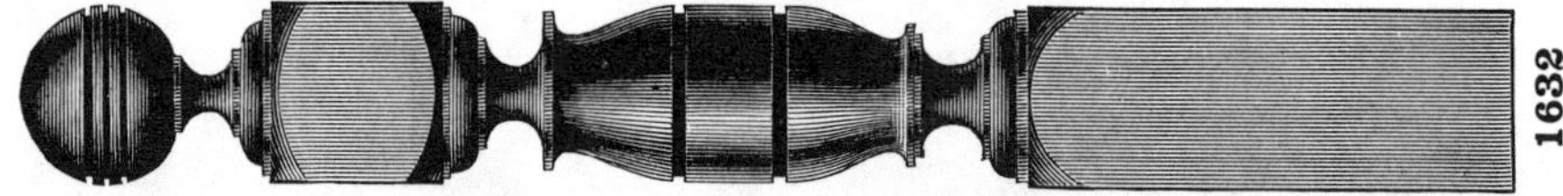

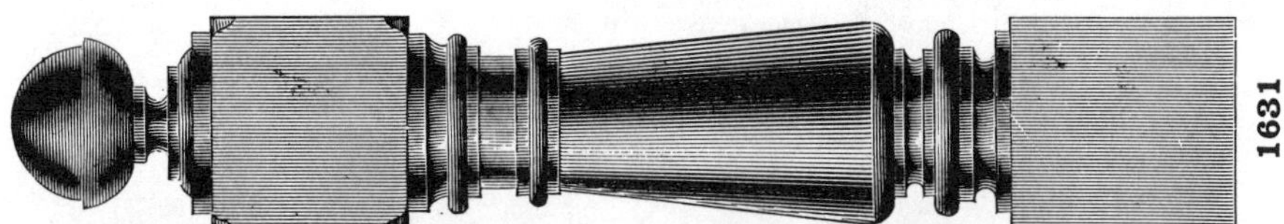

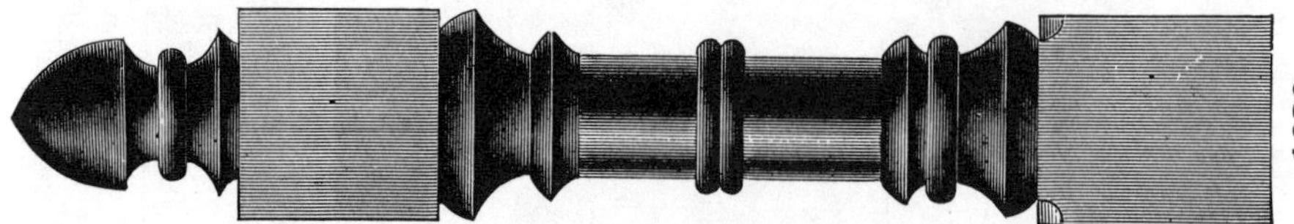

VERANDA POSTS.

1649

1650

1651

1652

1653

1654

OUTSIDE BALUSTERS.

1660

1661

1662

1663

1664

1665

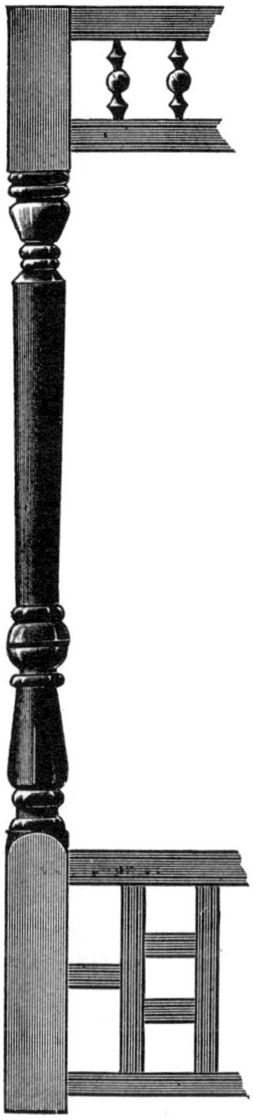

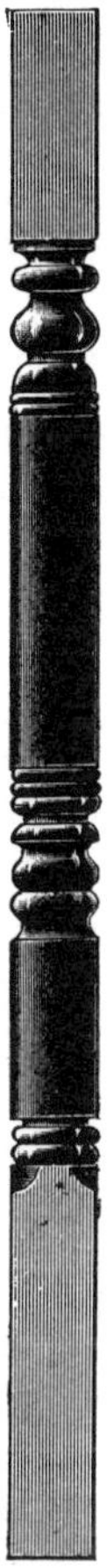

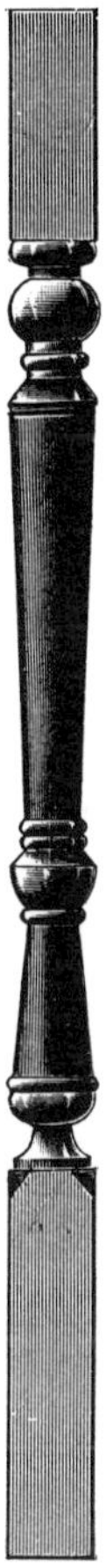

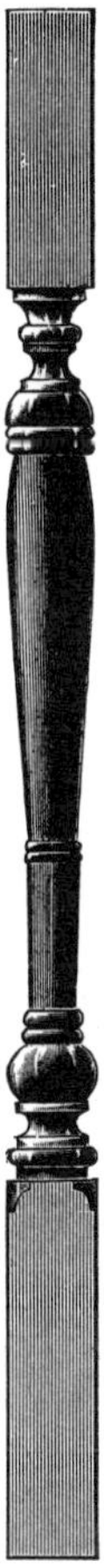

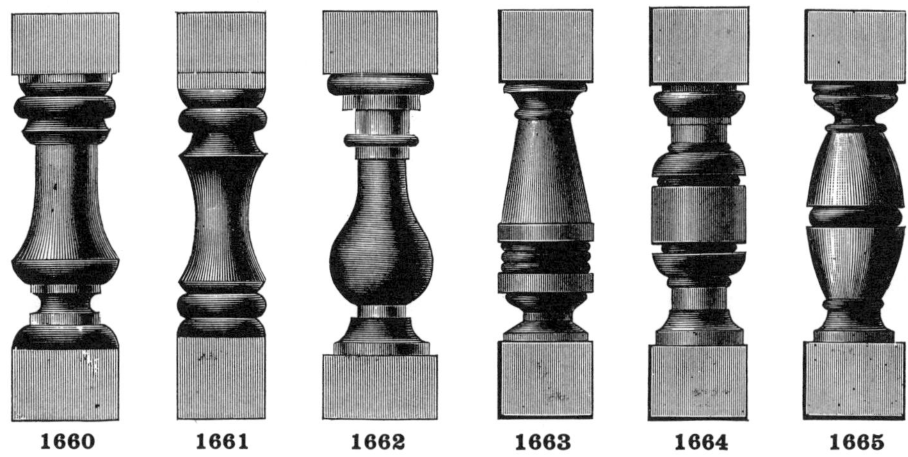

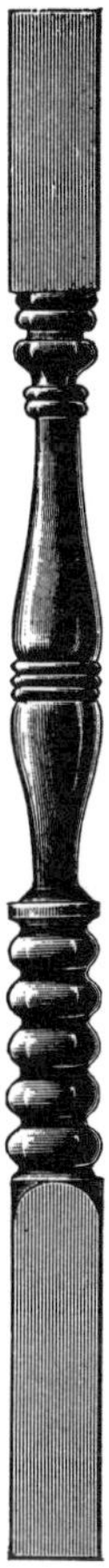

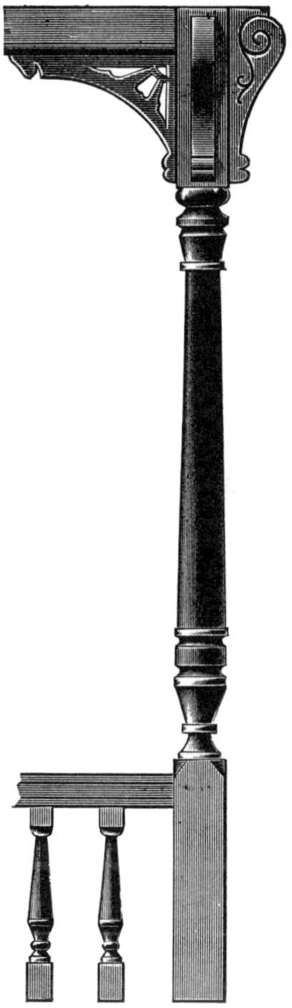

FOR PRICES SEE PAGE 9.

VERANDA POSTS.

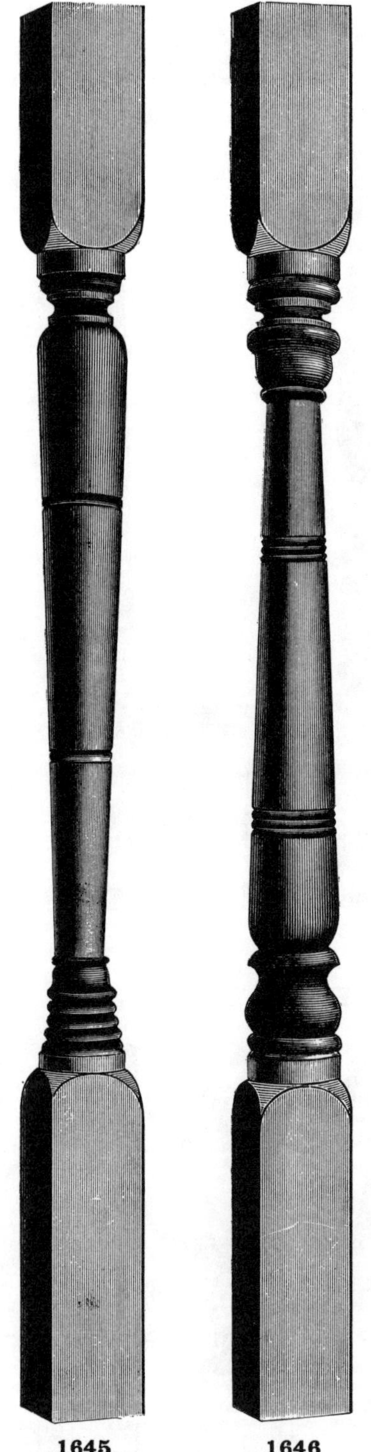

1645   1646

We have in stock Turned Poplar Columns No. 1646 as follows :

4 x 4 in.— 8 ft.   32 in. square at bottom, 20 in. square at top.   5 x 5 in.— 9 ft.   34 in. square at bottom, 22 in. square at top.
4 x 4 in.— 9 ft.   34 in. square at bottom, 22 in. square at top.   5 x 5 in.—10 ft.   36 in. square at bottom, 24 in. square at top.
4 x 4 in.—10 ft.   36 in. square at bottom, 24 in. square at top.   6 x 6 in.—10 ft.   36 in. square at bottom, 24 in. square at top.

The above are made of first quality seasoned poplar. Second quality Columns turned to order at reduced prices.

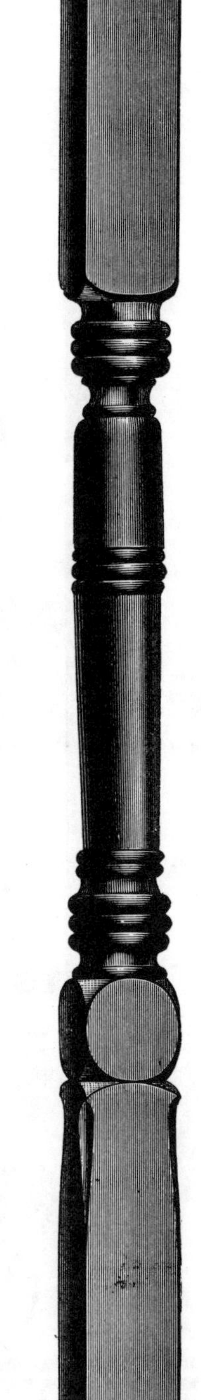

1648

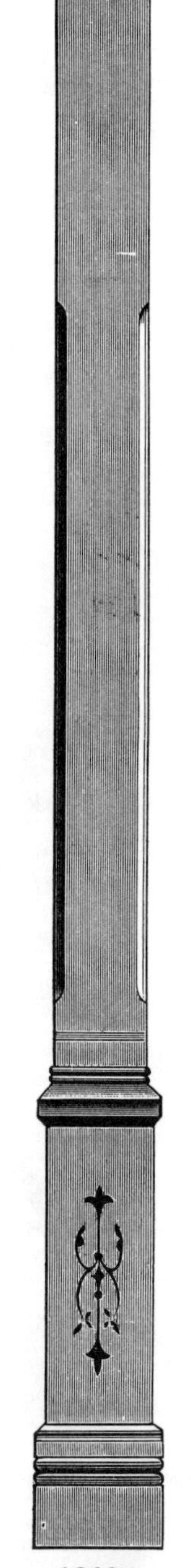

1648½

PORCH COLUMNS.

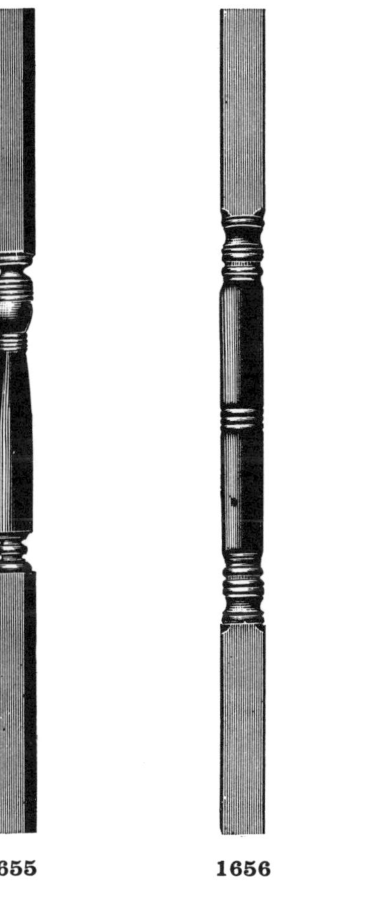

1655   1656   1657   1658

SPINDLES.

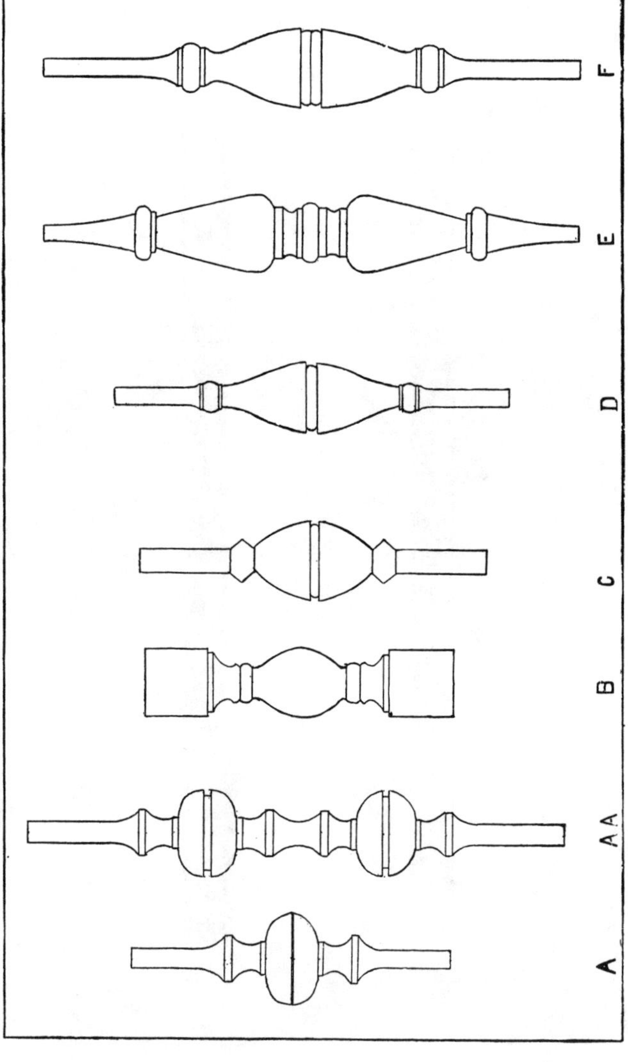

TURNED AND SAWED OUTSIDE BALUSTERS.

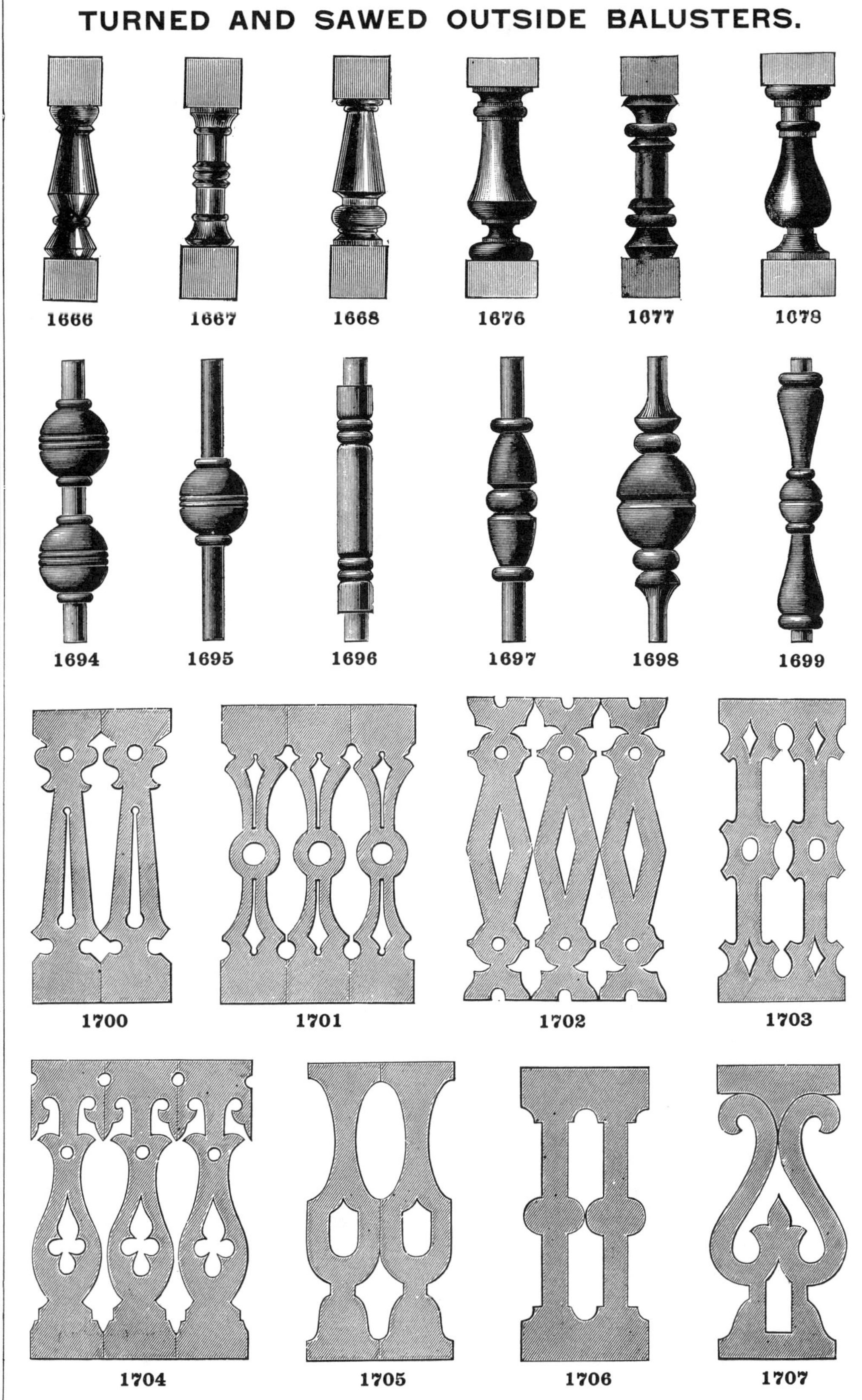

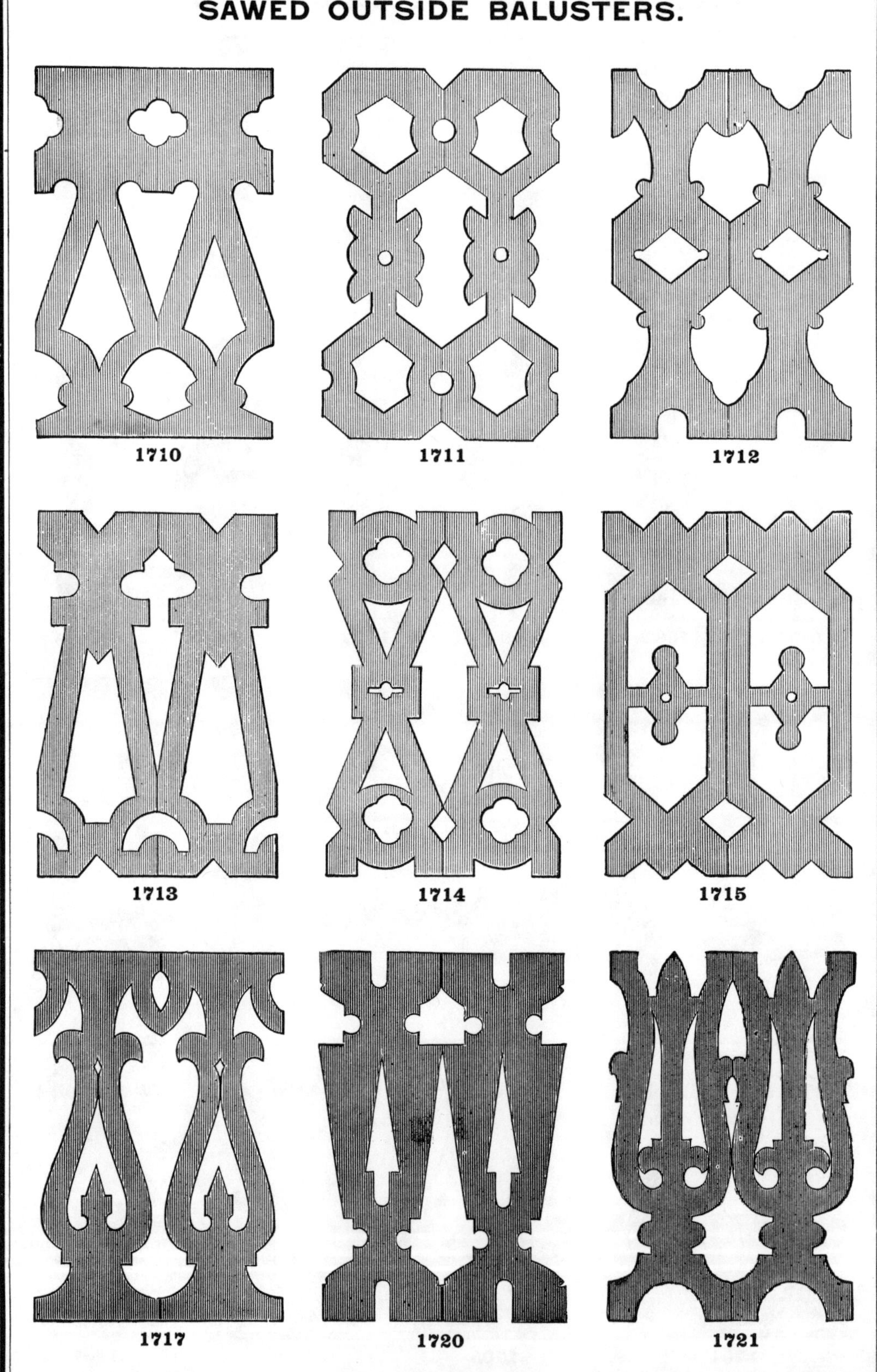

SAWED OUTSIDE BALUSTERS.
1710
1711
1712
1713
1714
1715
1717
1720
1721

VERANDAS.

1750

1751

1752

1753

VERANDAS.

1754

1755

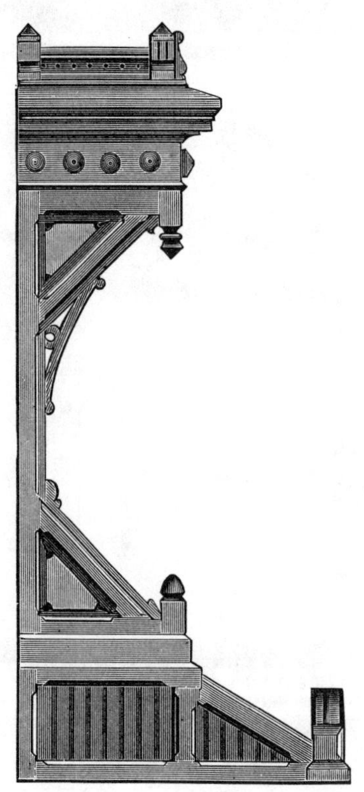

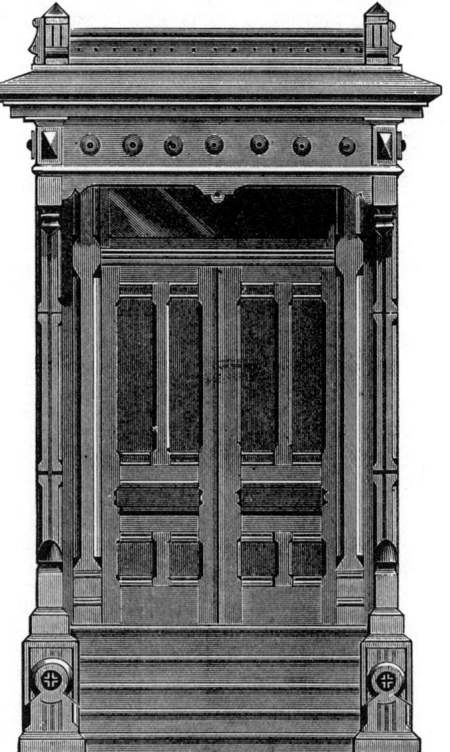

1756

WRITE FOR PRICES.

VERANDAS.

1757

1758

WRITE FOR PRICES.

VERANDAS.

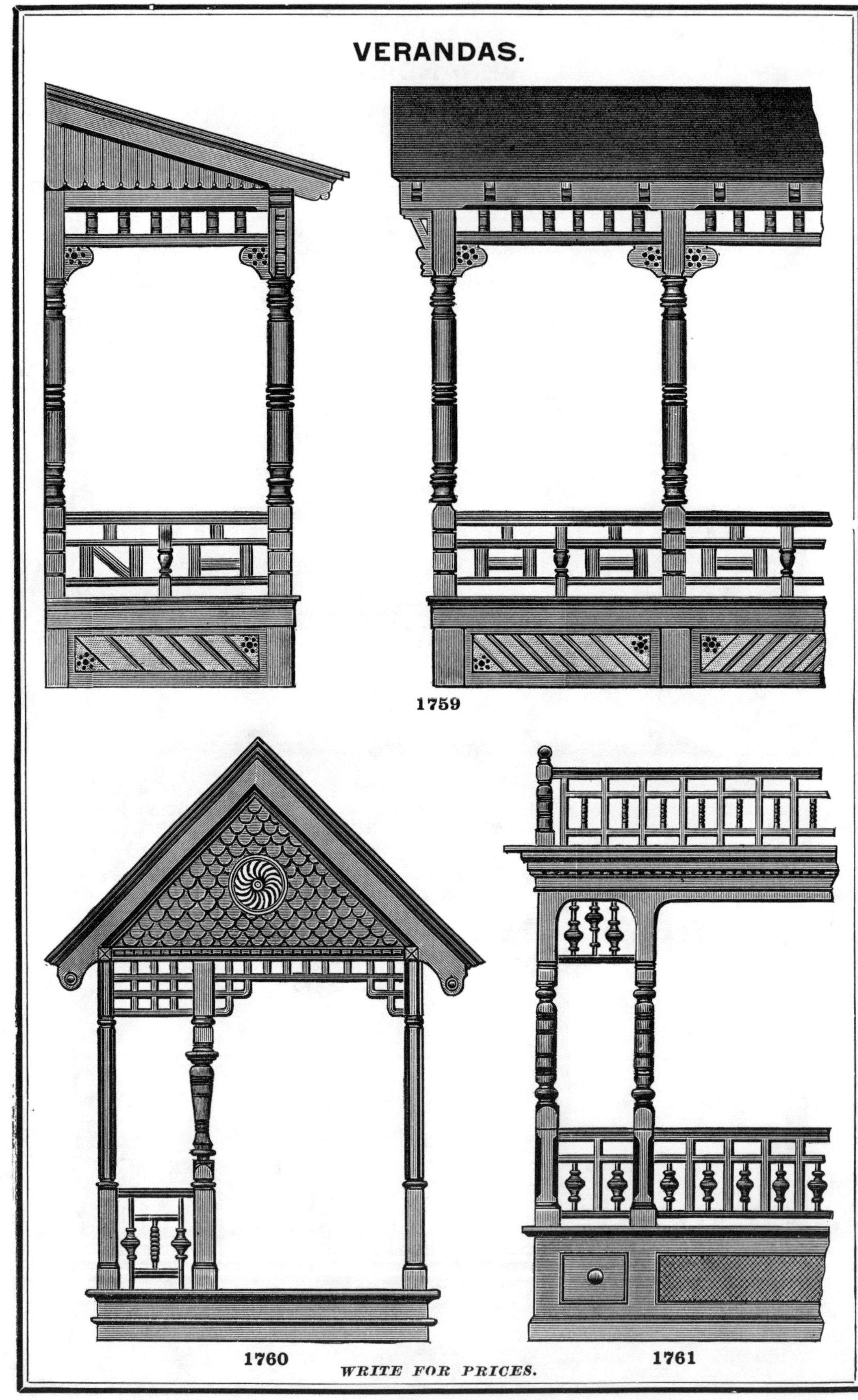

1759

1760   *WRITE FOR PRICES.*   1761

VERANDAS.

1771

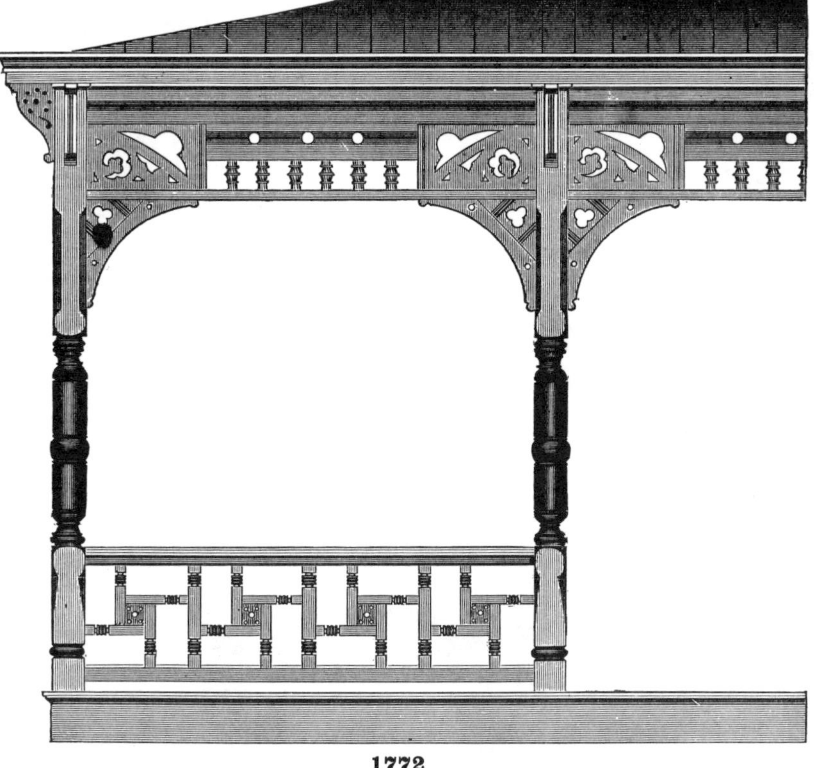

1772
WRITE FOR PRICES.

BRACKETS.

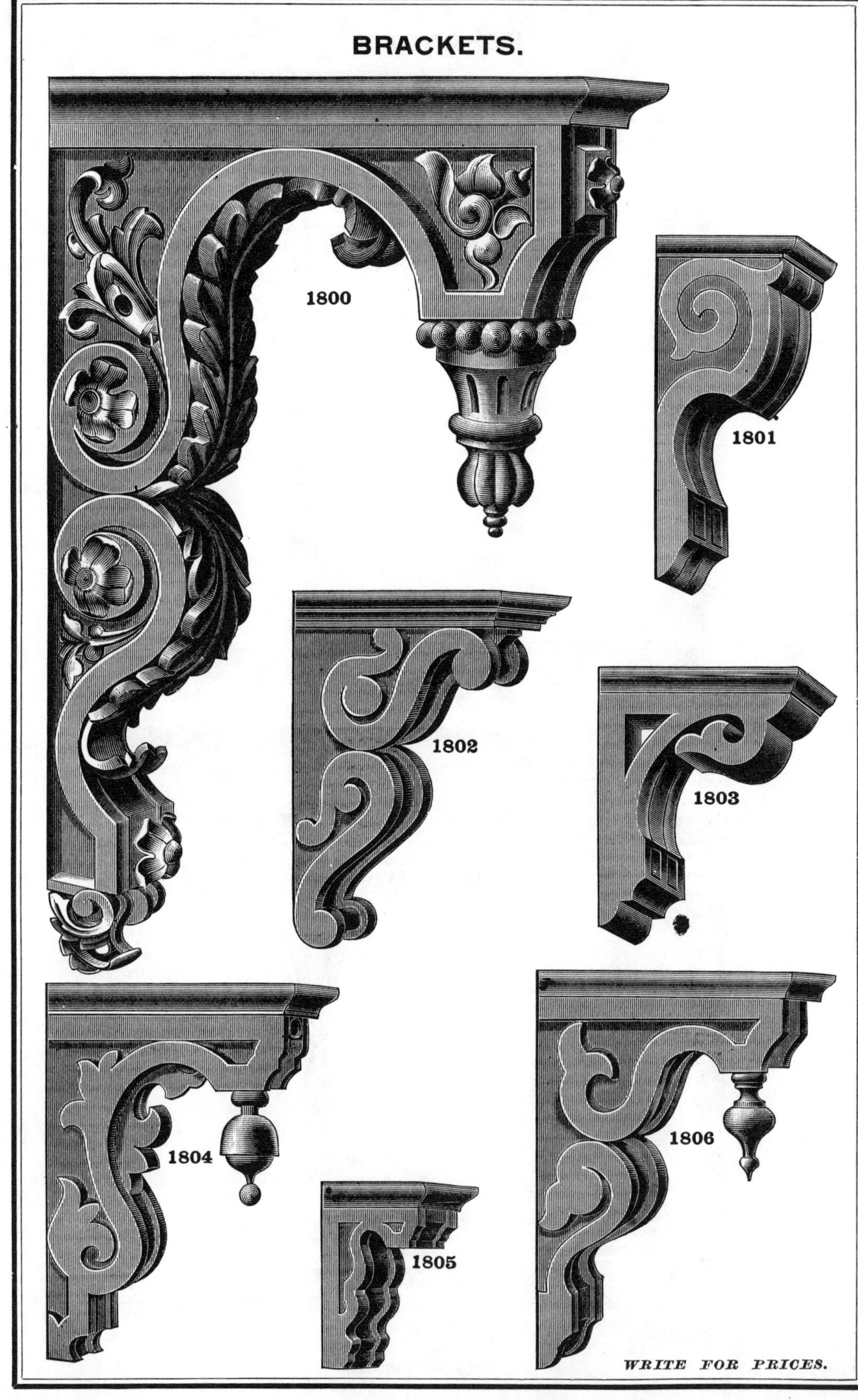

BRACKETS.

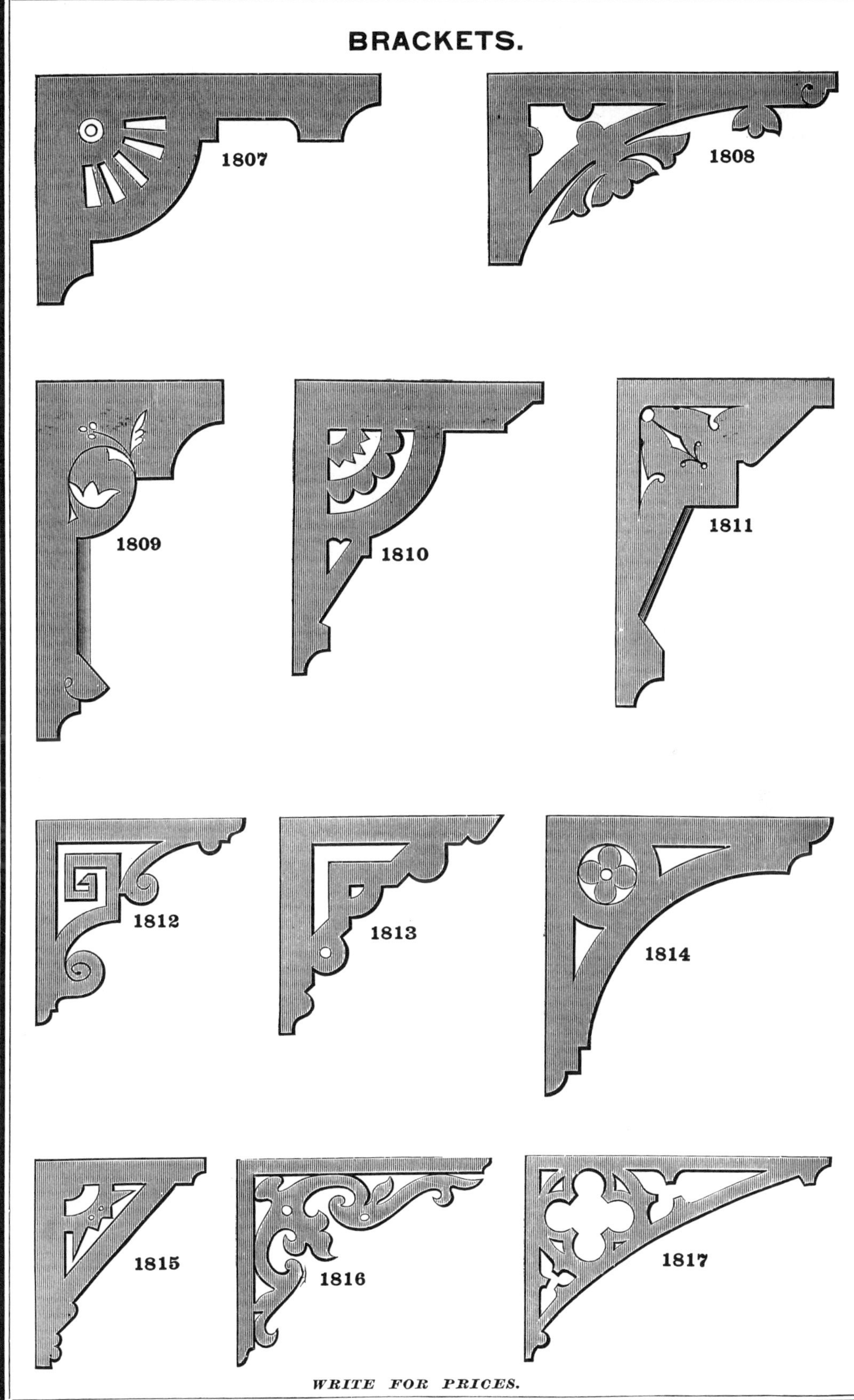

WRITE FOR PRICES.

BRACKETS.

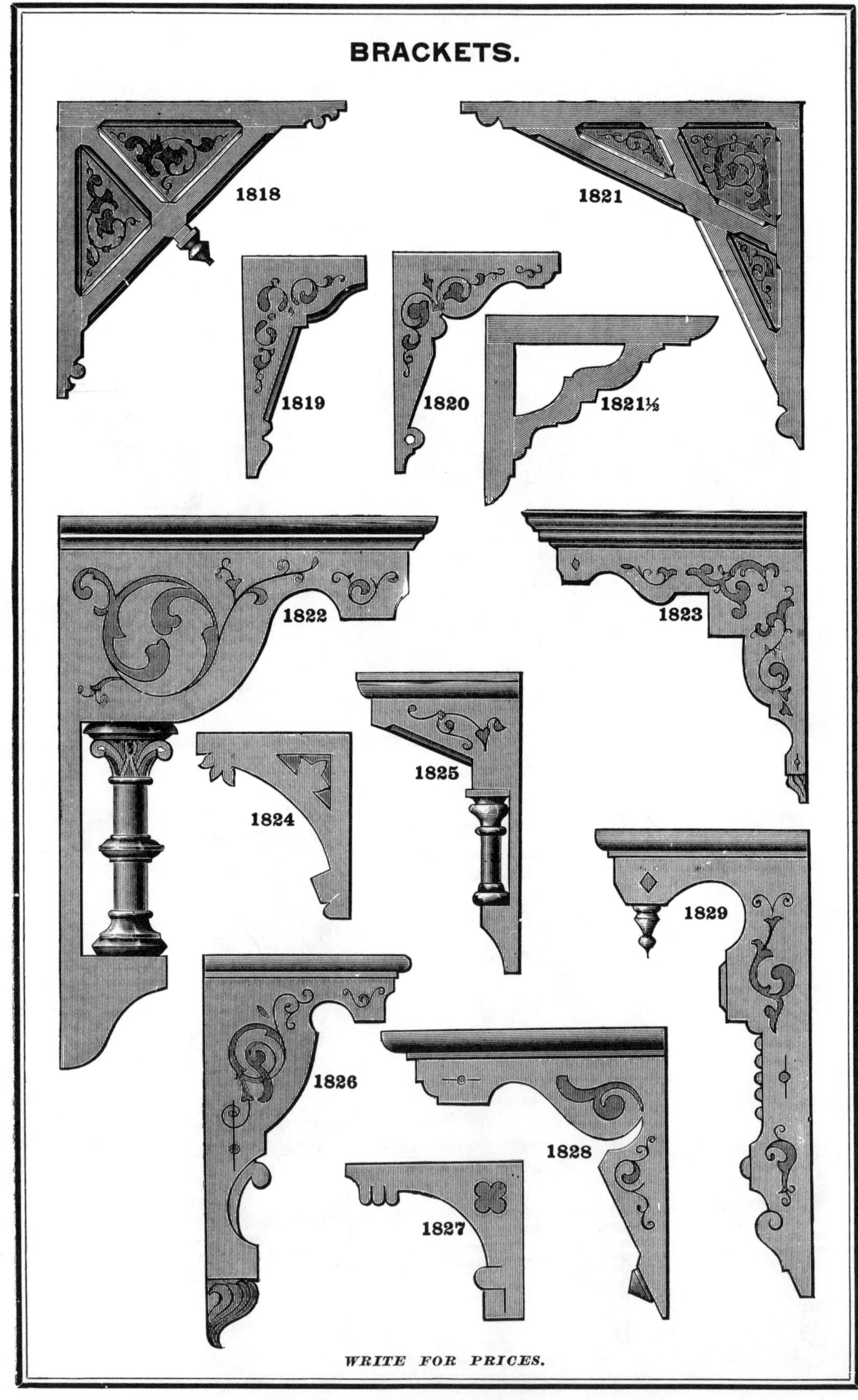

WRITE FOR PRICES.

BRACKETS.

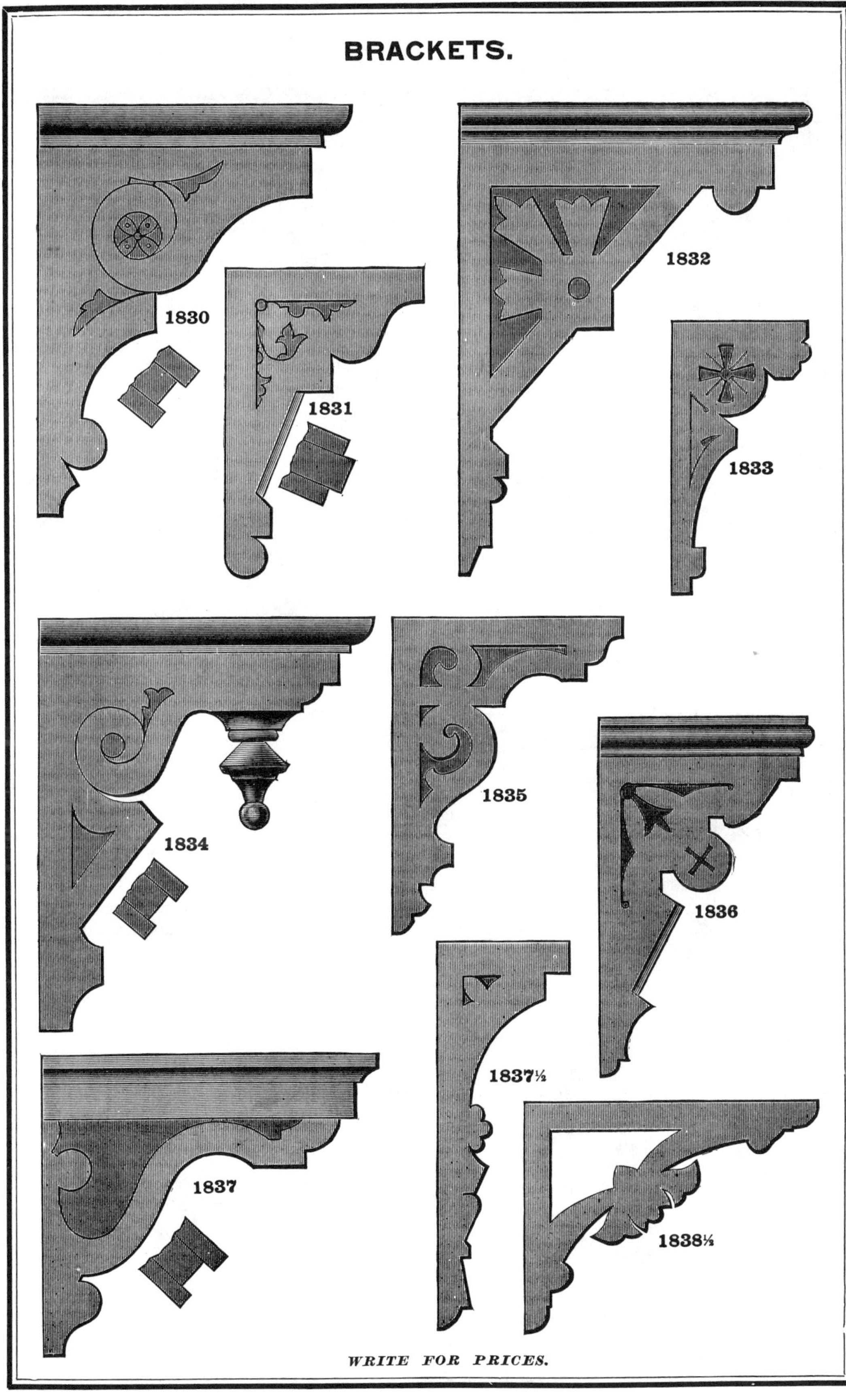

BRACKETS.

WRITE FOR PRICES.

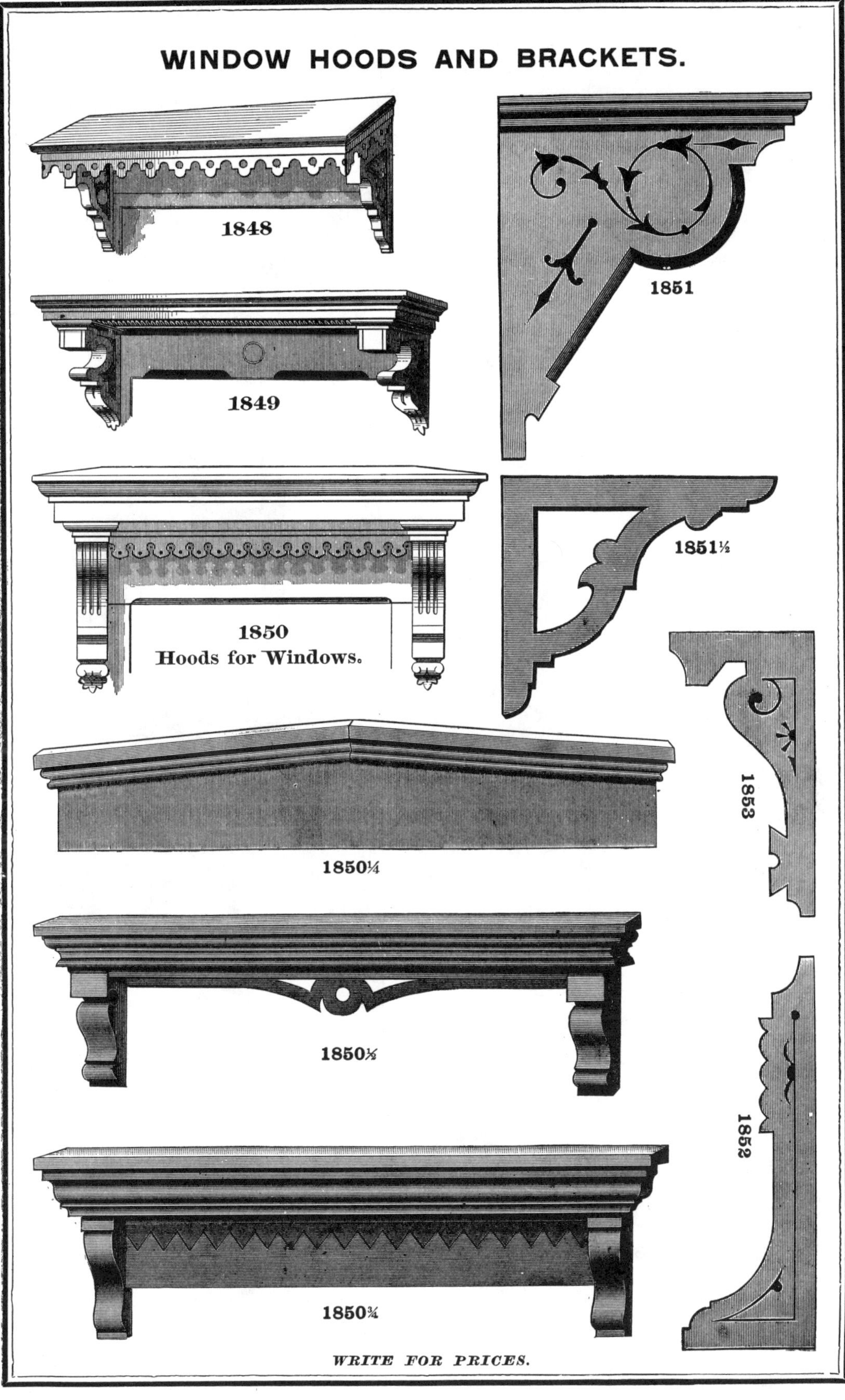

WINDOW HOODS AND BRACKETS.
1848
1849
1851
1850
Hoods for Windows.
1851½
1850¼
1853
1850½
1852
1850¾
WRITE FOR PRICES.

BRACKETS.

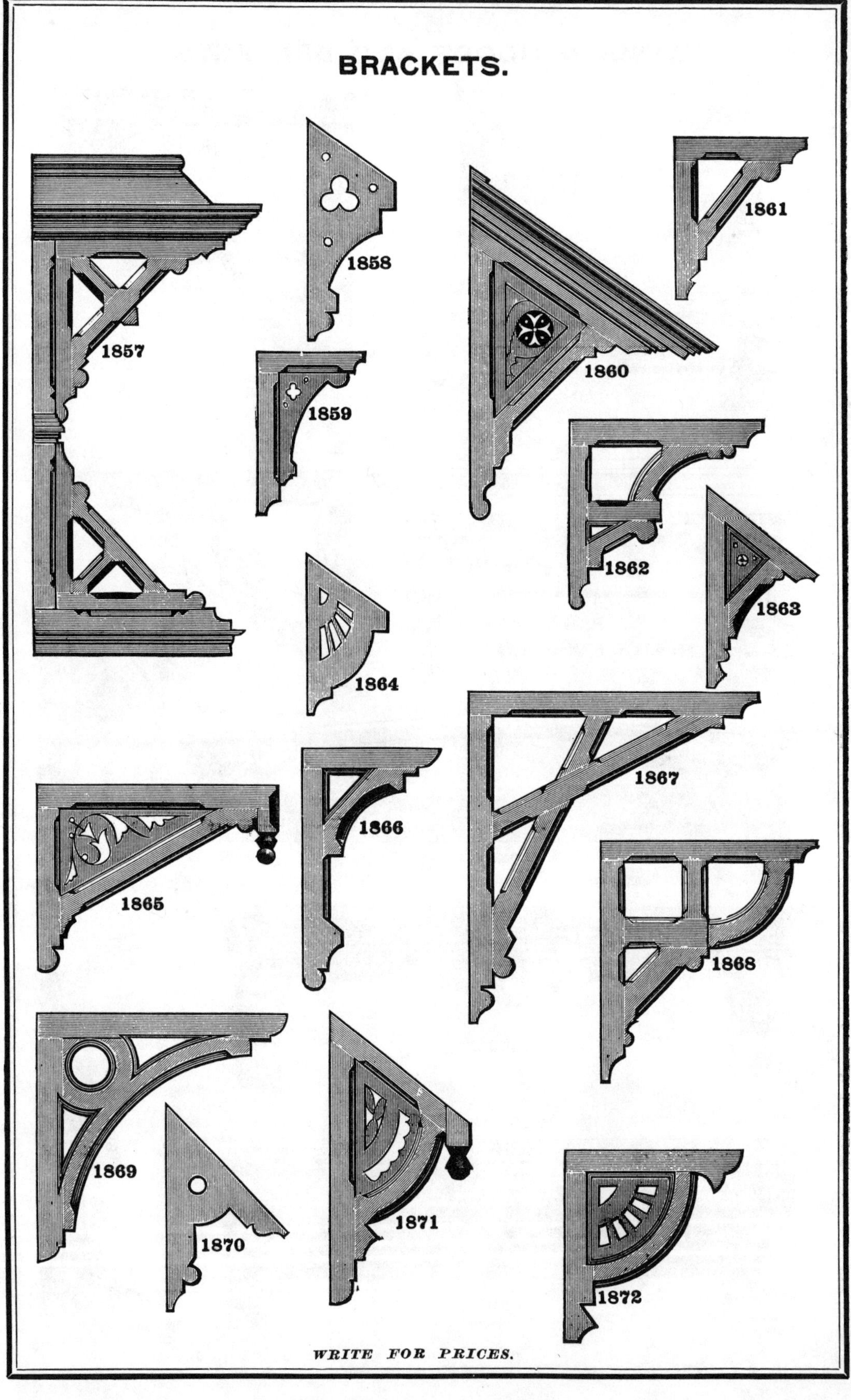

WRITE FOR PRICES.

BRACKETS.

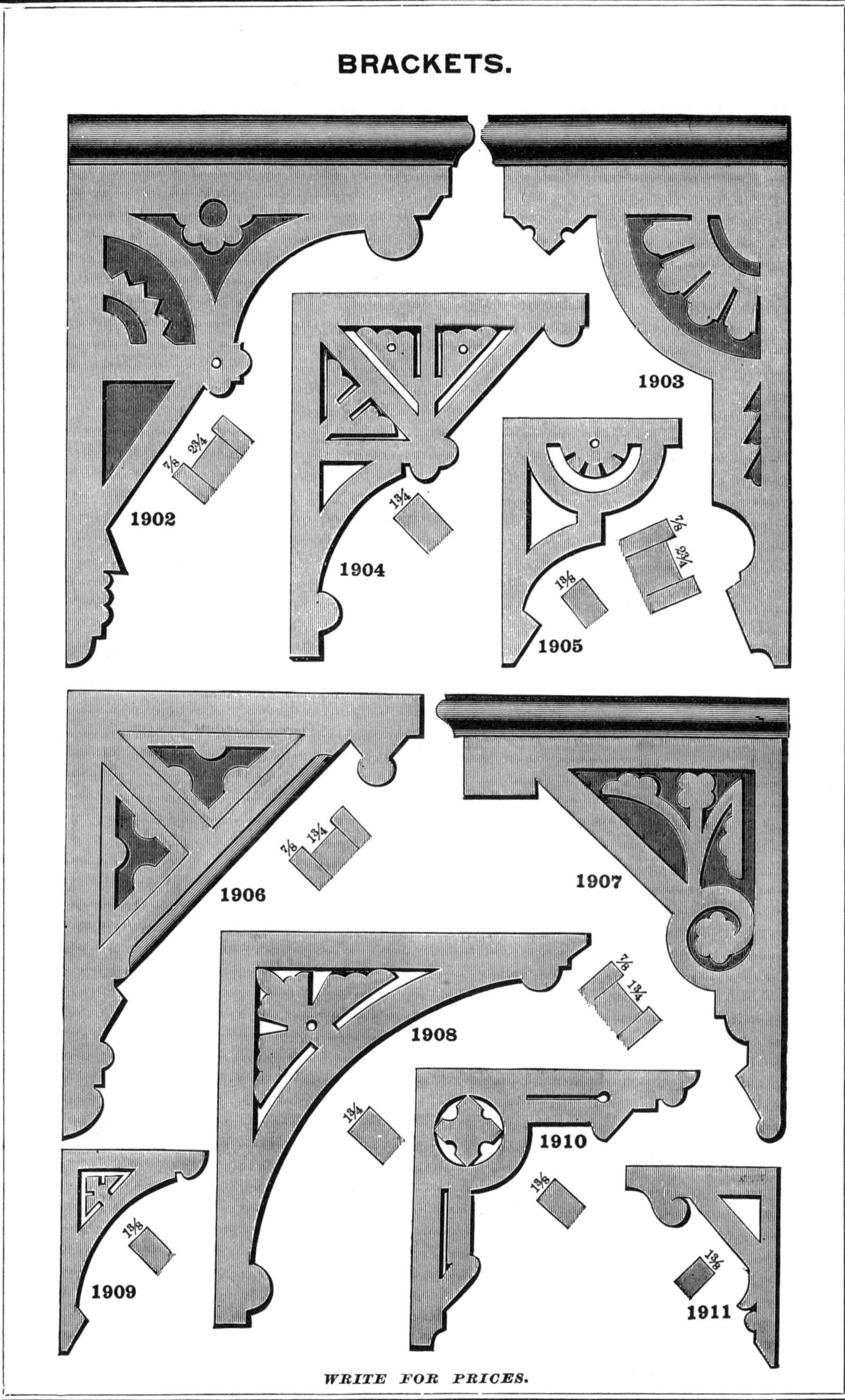

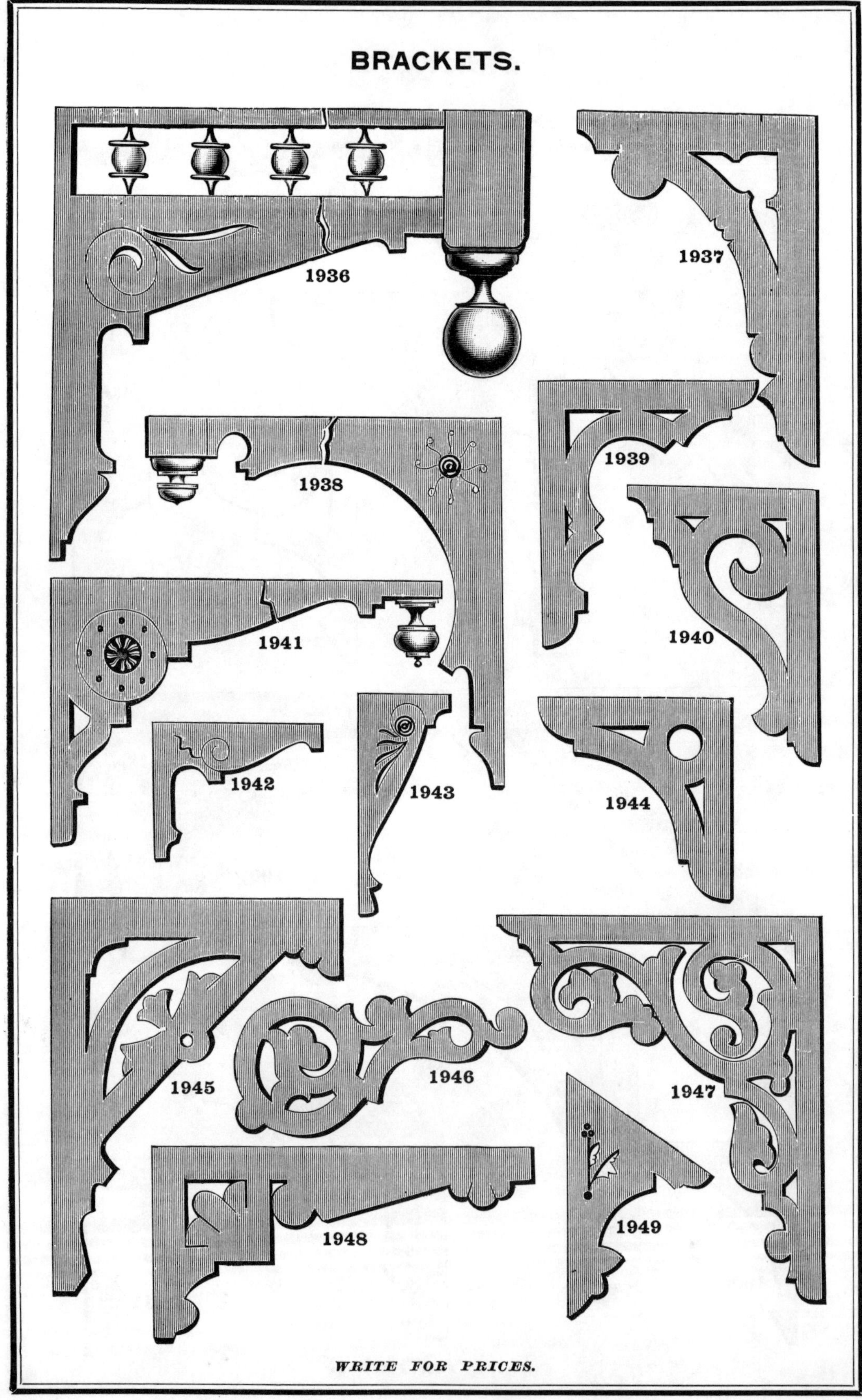

BRACKETS.
1936
1937
1938
1939
1940
1941
1942
1943
1944
1945
1946
1947
1948
1949
WRITE FOR PRICES.

GABLE FINISH.

WRITE FOR PRICES.

CORNICE DRAPERY, VERGE BOARDS, ETC.

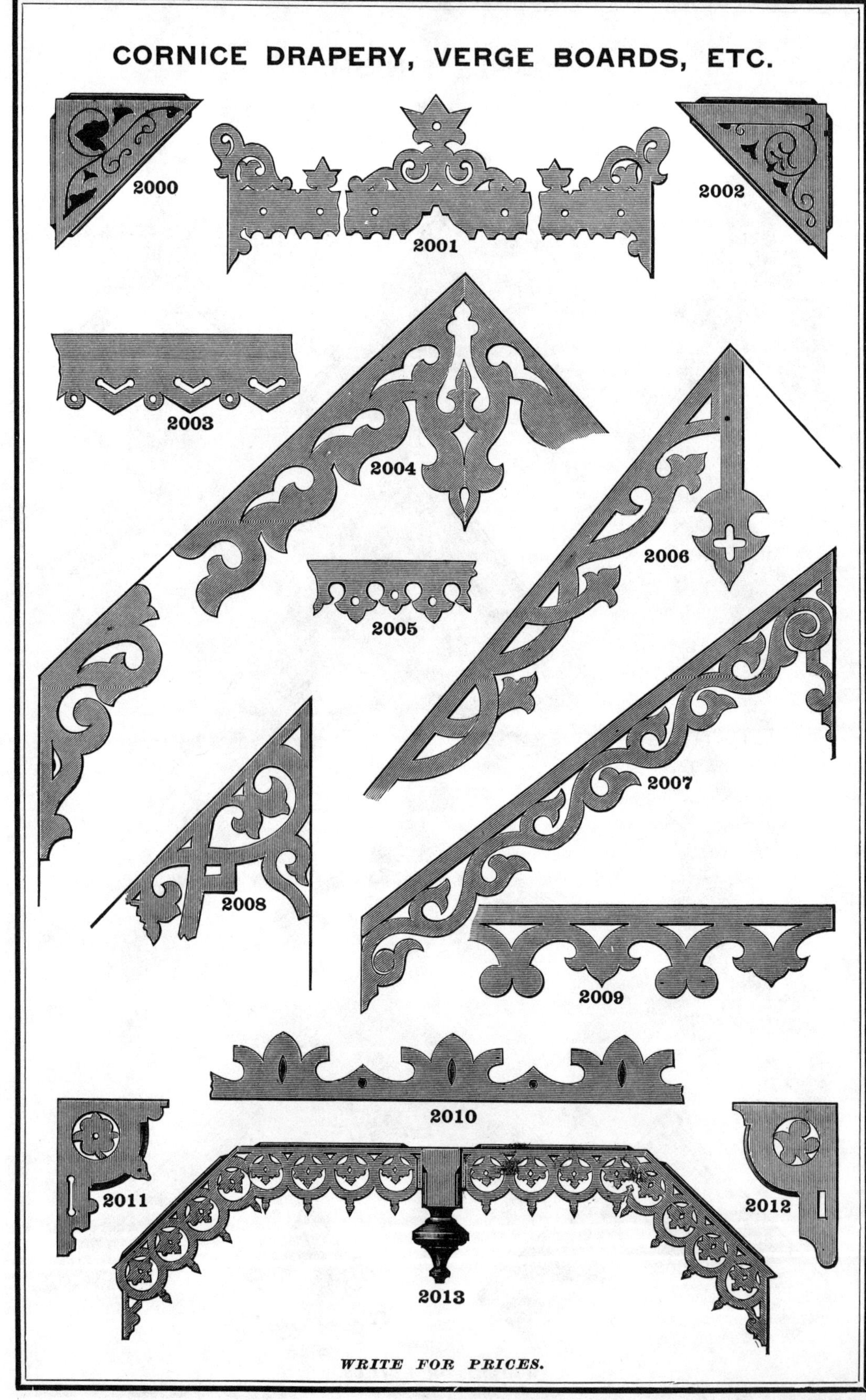

WRITE FOR PRICES.

GABLE FINISH AND WOOD ROSETTES.

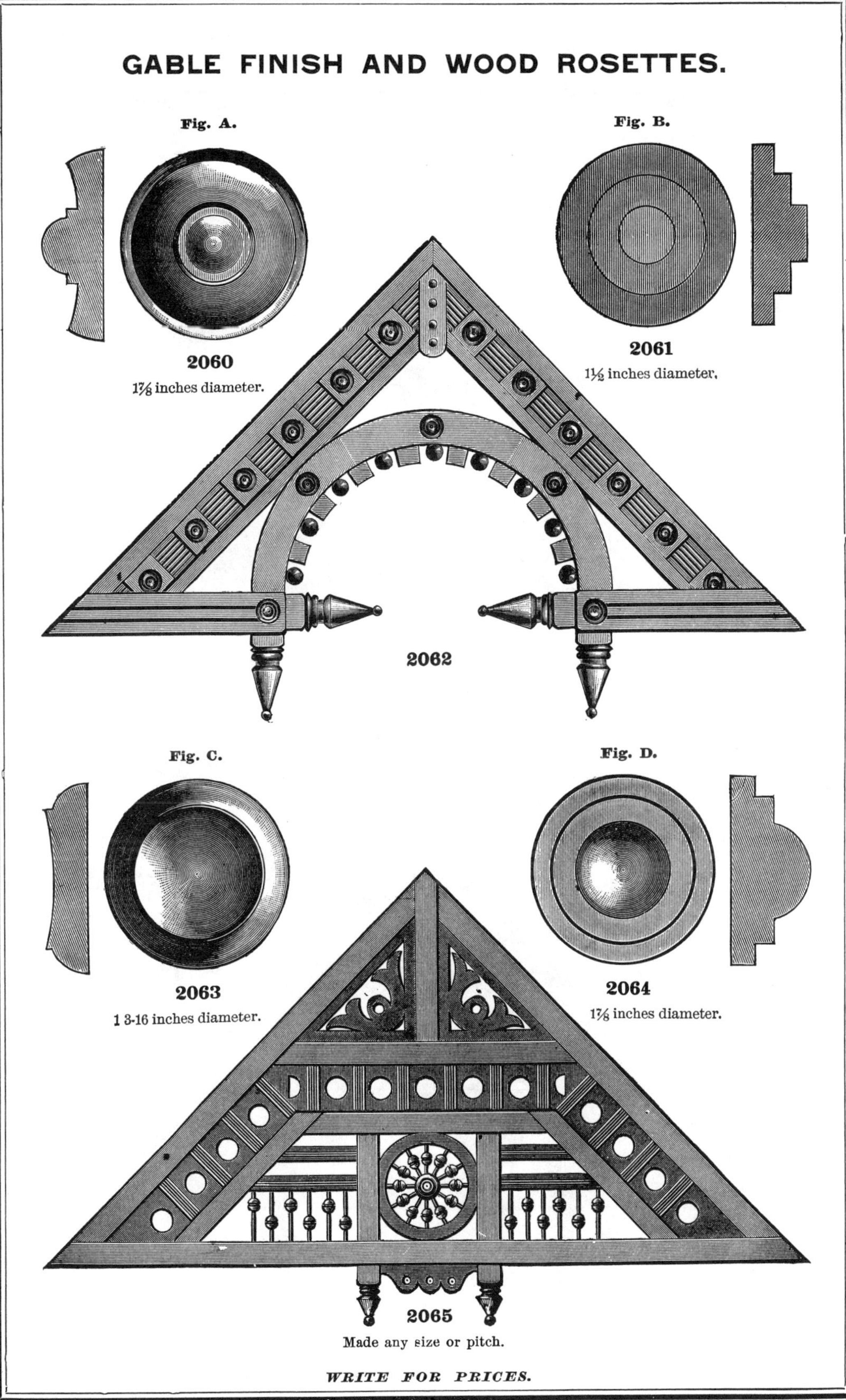

WRITE FOR PRICES.

GABLE FINISH AND WOOD ROSETTES.

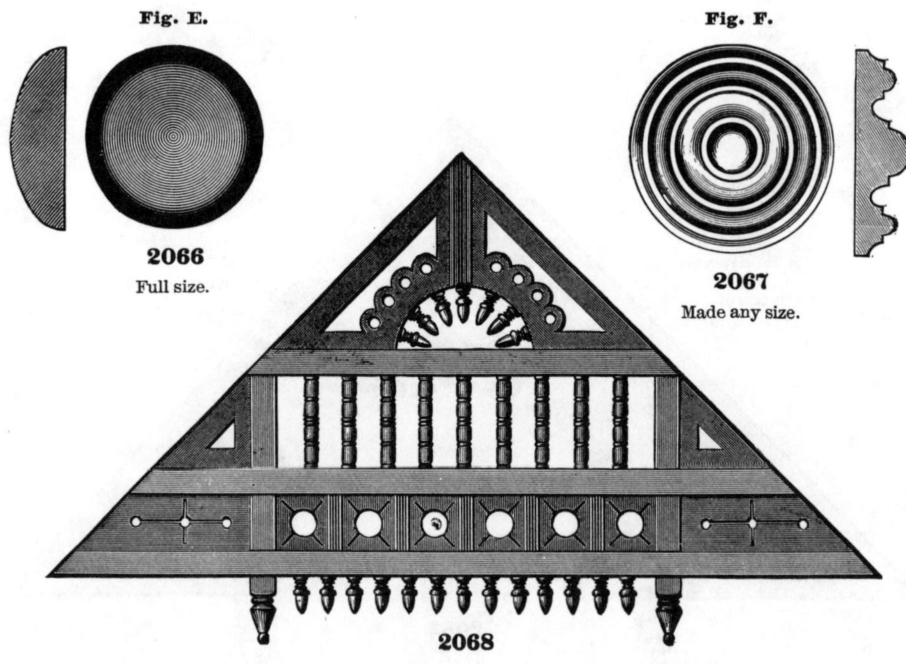

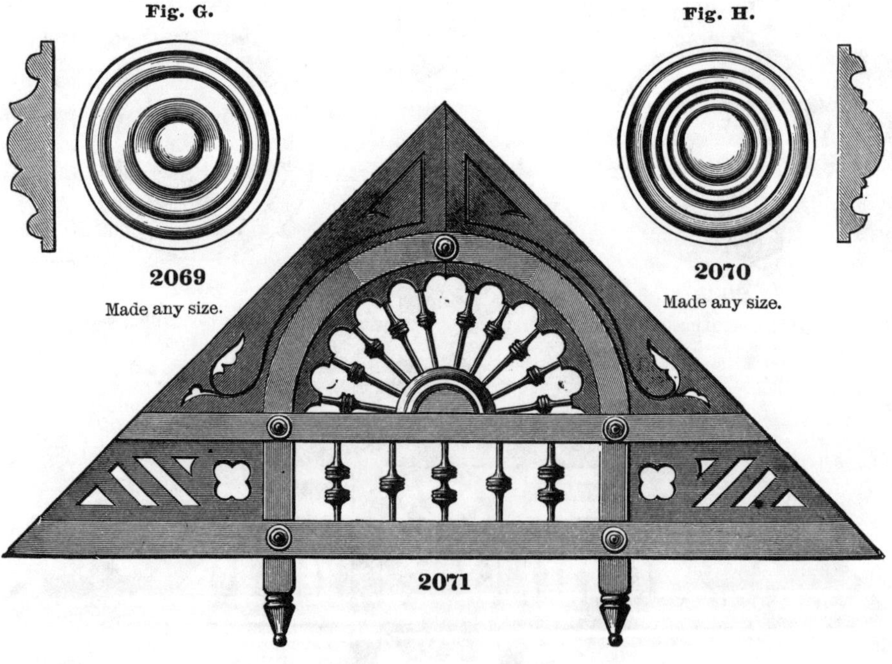

WRITE FOR PRICES.

GABLE FINISH AND WOOD ROSETTES.

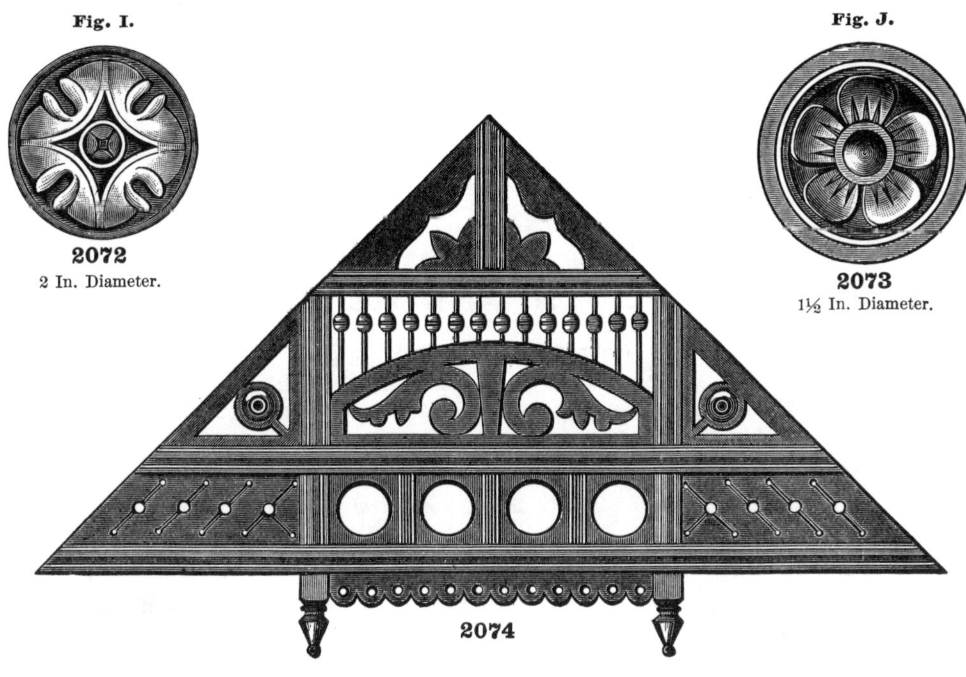

Fig. I.

2072
2 In. Diameter.

Fig. J.

2073
1½ In. Diameter.

2074

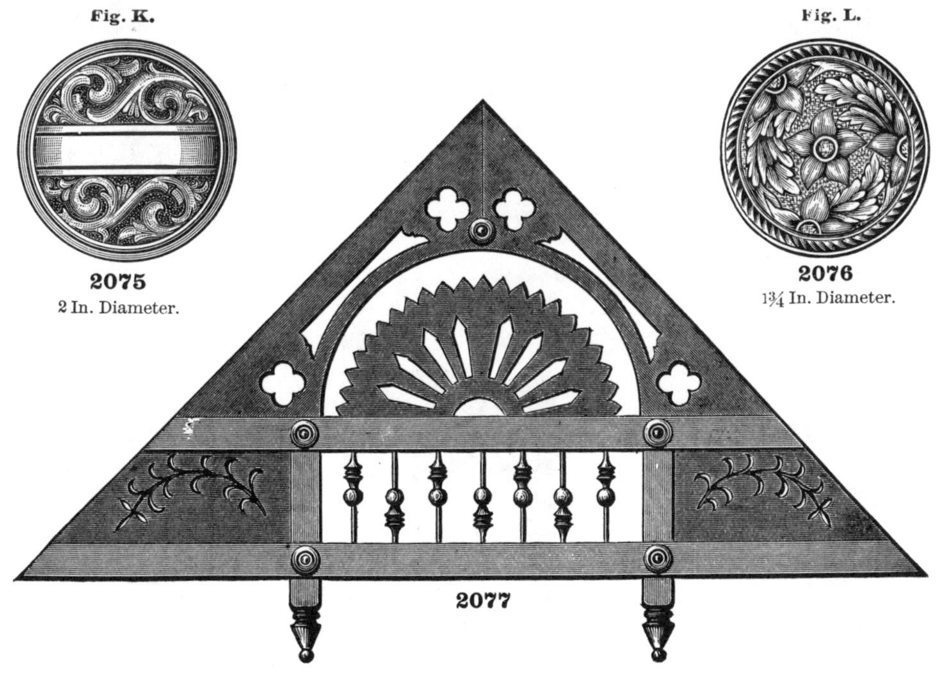

Fig. K.

2075
2 In. Diameter.

Fig. L.

2076
1¾ In. Diameter.

2077

Made any size or pitch.

WRITE FOR PRICES.

CORNER AND BASE BEADS.

Corner Bead, No. **690**
1⅜ inch and 1¾ inch, 4 feet long, carried in stock.

Base Bead, No. **698**
1⅜ × 12½.

Base Bead, No. **699**
1⅜ × 14½.

CORNER, PLINTH, AND HEAD BLOCKS.

We manufacture *CORNER AND PLINTH BLOCKS* in a great variety of patterns, and give following a few cuts of styles with prices. The prices given are for *White and Yellow Pine* by the hundred. Red Oak or Birch are 50 per cent. higher, and Walnut 100 per cent. higher than marked prices. We also furnish *Carved* Corner or Plinth Blocks in endless varieties, at a small additional cost over those turned.

☞ *We sell Blocks in quantity desired. A liberal Discount to Dealers.*

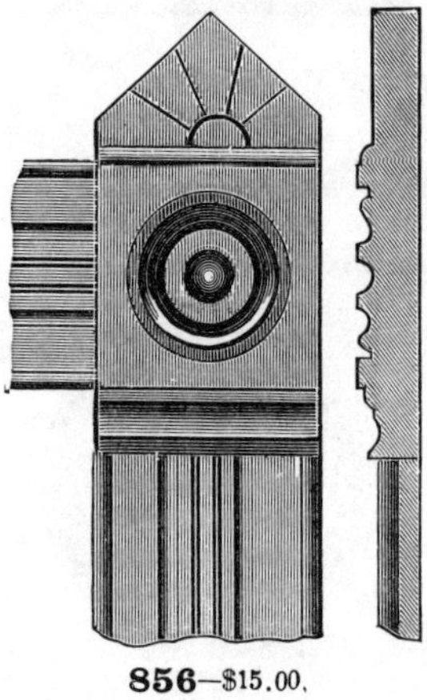

856—$15.00. **780**—$5.00.  **855**—$50.00.

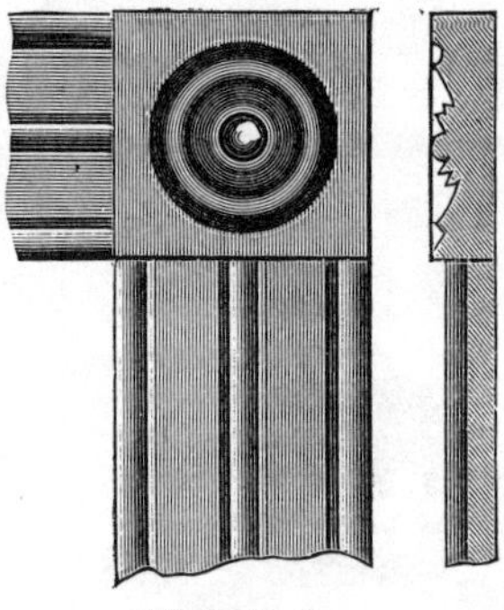

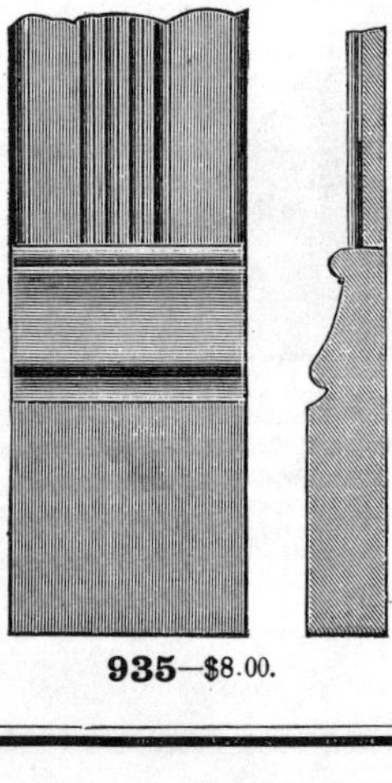

935—$8.00. **936**—$20.00.  **937**—$9.00.

WOOD CORNER BLOCKS.

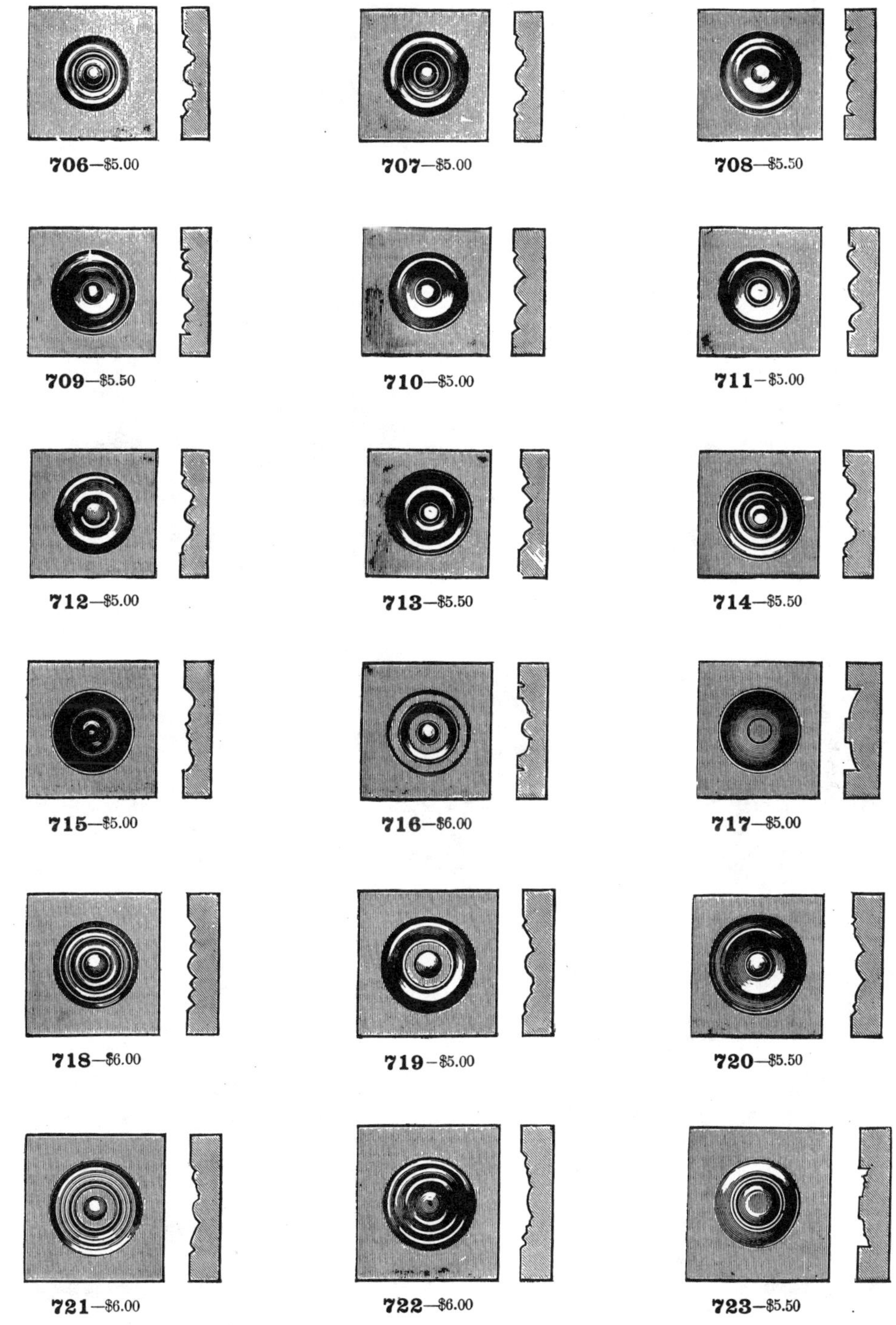

706—$5.00

707—$5.00

708—$5.50

709—$5.50

710—$5.00

711—$5.00

712—$5.00

713—$5.50

714—$5.50

715—$5.00

716—$6.00

717—$5.00

718—$6.00

719—$5.00

720—$5.50

721—$6.00

722—$6.00

723—$5.50

Above prices are for Blocks from 4×4 to $6 \times 6 \times 1\frac{1}{8}$ inches thick.
Prices are for White Pine by the hundred.

WOOD CORNER BLOCKS.

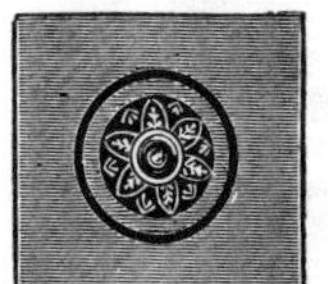

724

4½ to 6 in. $10.00

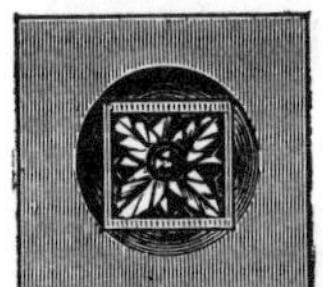

725

4½ to 6 in. $10.00

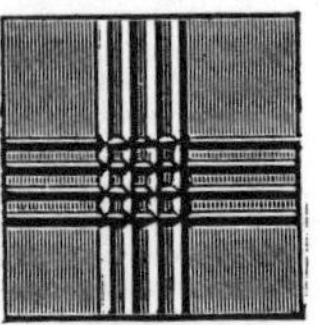

726

4½ to 6 in. $7.00

727

4½ to 6 in. $7.00

728

4½ to 6 in. $20.00

729

4½ to 6 in. $20.00

730

4½ to 6 in. $7.00

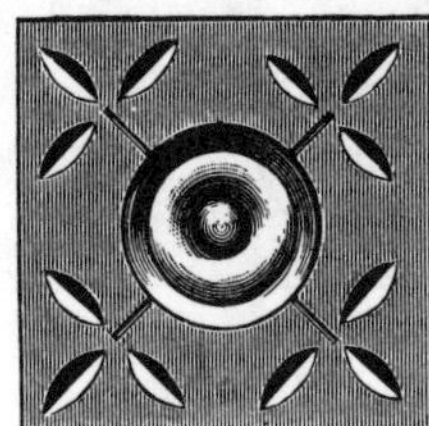

731

4½ to 6 in. $6.50

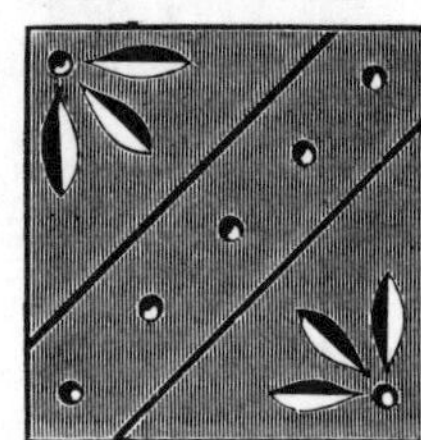

732

4½ to 6 in. $5.50

733

4½ to 6 in. $20.00

734

4½ to 6 in. $20.00

Prices are for White Pine by the hundred for Blocks 1⅛ inches thick.

WOOD CORNER BLOCKS.

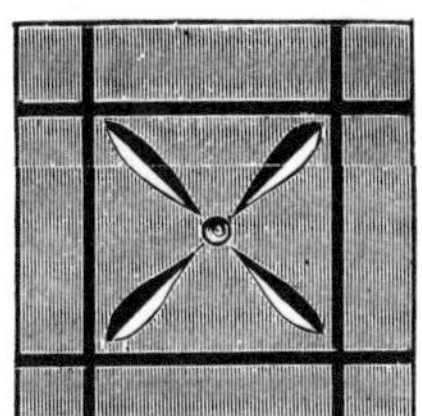

735
4½ to 6 in. × 1⅛, $5.50

736
4½ to 6 in. × 1⅛, $6.50

736½
4¼ to 6 in. × 1⅛, $6.00

737
4½ to 6 in. × 1⅛, $6.50

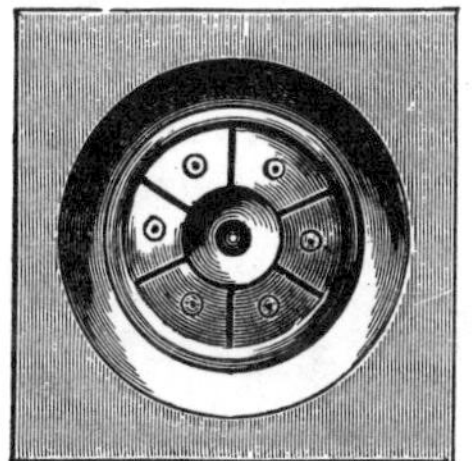

739
4½ to 6 in. × 1⅛, $6.50

738
4½ to 6 in. × 1⅛, $5.50

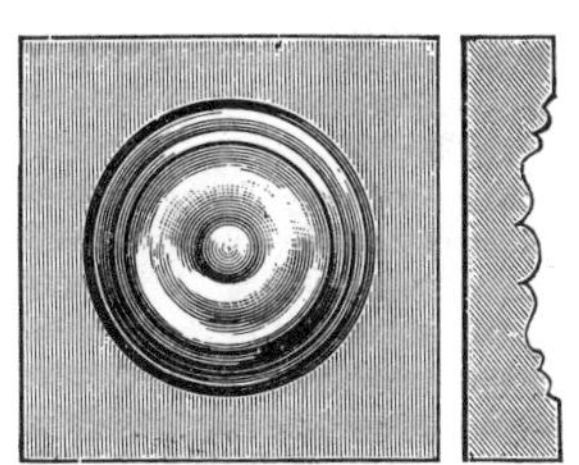

740
4½ to 6 in. × 1⅛, $5.50

741
4½ to 6 in. × 1⅛, $25.00

742
4½ to 6 in. × 1⅛, $8.50

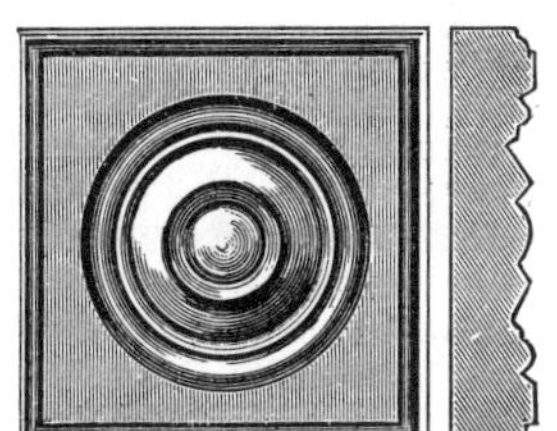

743
4½ to 6 in. × 1⅛, $7.00

744
4½ to 6 in. × 1⅛, Hand Carved, $110.00

745
4½ to 6 in. × 1⅛, $6.50

WOOD CORNER BLOCKS.

747

4½ to 6 × 1⅛, $25.00

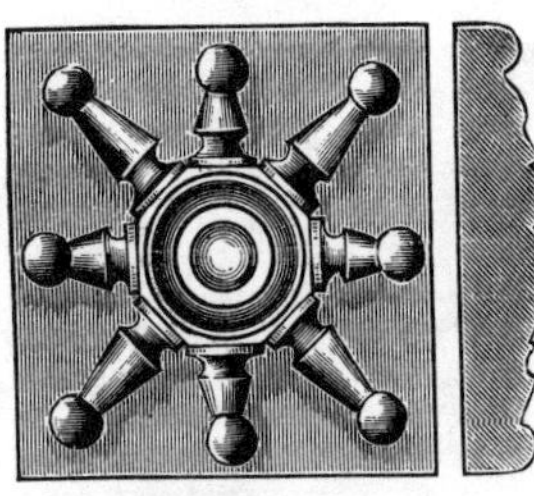

748

4½ to 6 × 1⅛, $18.00

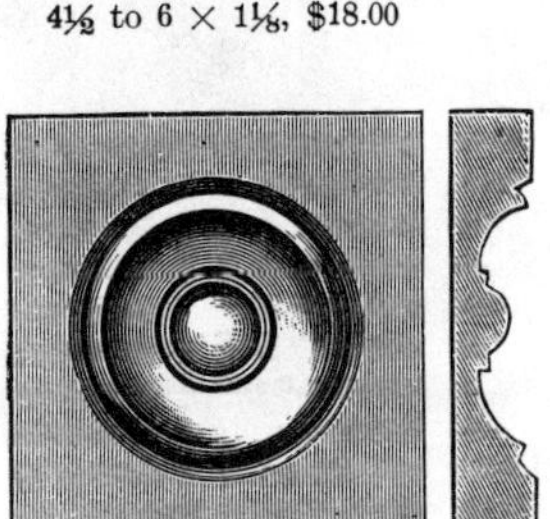

749

4½ to 6 × 1⅛, $5.00

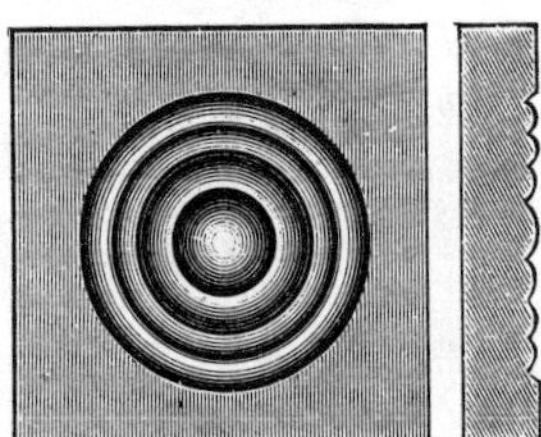

750

4½ to 6 × 1⅛, $5.50

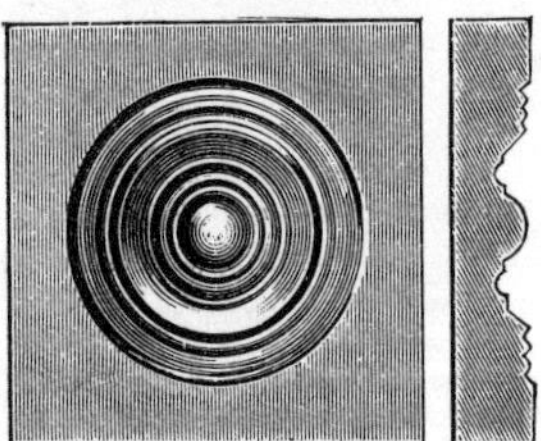

751

4½ to 6 × 1⅛, $6.00

752

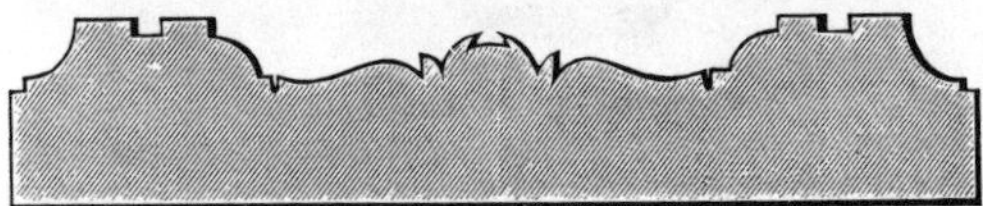

SIZE.	Thickness.	Price per 100.
4½ to 5¾ In. Square.	1⅛	$15.00
6 to 6¾ " "	"	18.00
5 to 5¾ " "	1⅜	18.00
6 to 6¾ " "	"	20.00

753

Prices same as No. 752 above.

WOOD CORNER BLOCKS AND ORNAMENTS.

754

1⅝ × 8, $12.50 per 100

756

SIZE.	Thickness.	Price per 100.
4½ to 5¾ In. Square.	1⅛	$15.00
6 to 6¾ " "	"	18.00
5 to 5¾ " "	1⅜	18.00
6 to 6¾ " "	"	20 00

755

3⅛ × 2½, $8.00 per 100
2¾ × 4½, $13.00 per 100

757

Sizes and prices same as No. 756.

WOOD CORNER BLOCKS AND ORNAMENTS.

758

Price same as No. 756.

759

SIZE.	Thickness.	Price per 100.
5 to 6 In. Square	1⅛	$25.00
6 to 6¾ " "	1⅜	30.00
7 to 8½ " "	"	35.00
6 to 6¾ " "	1¾	35.00
7 to 8¼ " "	"	38.00

760

4 In. Diameter. $18.00 per 100

761

3¾ In. Square. $18.00 per 100
4¾ In. Square.   25.00 per 100

762

2¾ × 6 In. $25.00 per 100
3¾ × 8 In.   30.00 per 100

WOOD ORNAMENTS.

763

764

765

766

767

768

769

770

771

PRICES OF ABOVE ORNAMENTS.

No.	Size.	Per 100.	No.	Size.	Per 100.
763	1 inches diameter.	$1.50	765	2⅜ inches square.	$ 5.50
763	1¼ " "	2.00	766	1⅞ " "	4.25
763	1½ " "	2 50	767	1¾ " diameter.	3.00
763	1¾ " "	3.00	768	1⅞ " square.	4.25
763	2 " "	3.75	768	2⅜ " "	6.00
763	2¼ " "	4.50	768	3¼ " "	15.00
763	2½ " "	5.50	769	1¾ " "	3.75
763	2¾ " "	6.50	770	1¾ " diameter.	3.00
763	3¼ " "	7.50	770	2½ " "	6.50
764	1 " "	2.00	771	1⅛ " "	2.00
764	1¼ " "	3.00	771	1⅜ " "	2.50
764	1½ " "	3.75	771	1⅝ " "	3 00
764	1¾ " "	4.25	771	2¼ " "	4.50
764	2 " "	4.50			

WOOD CORNER BLOCKS.

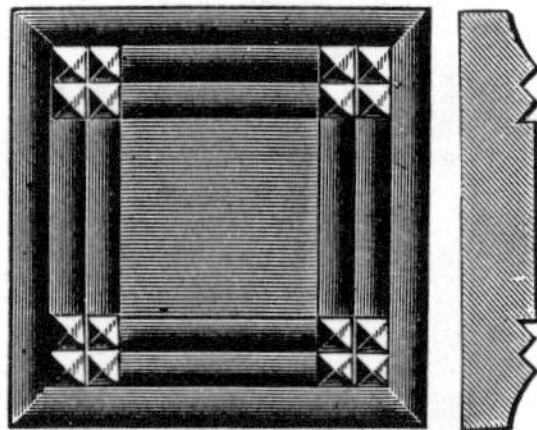

776

4½ to 6 in. sq. × 1⅜ $9.00 per 100

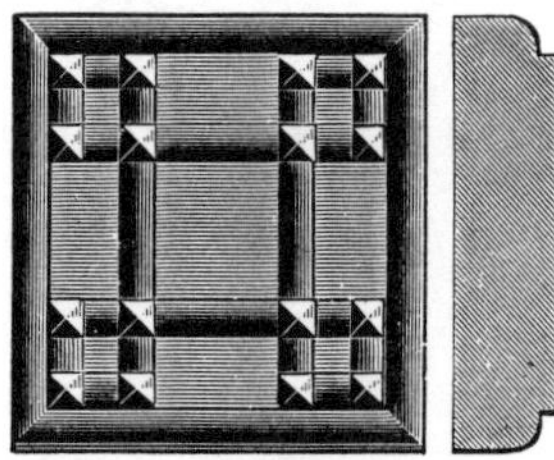

777

4½ to 6 in. sq. × 1⅜ $15.00 per 100

778

4½ to 6 in. sq. × 1⅛ $10.00 per 100

779

4½ to 6 in. sq. × 1⅛ $20.00 per 100

787

5 to 6 in. sq. × 1⅛ $15.00 per 100

788

5 to 6 in. sq. × 1⅛ $25.00 per 100

791

5 to 6 in. sq. × 1⅛ $10.00 per 100

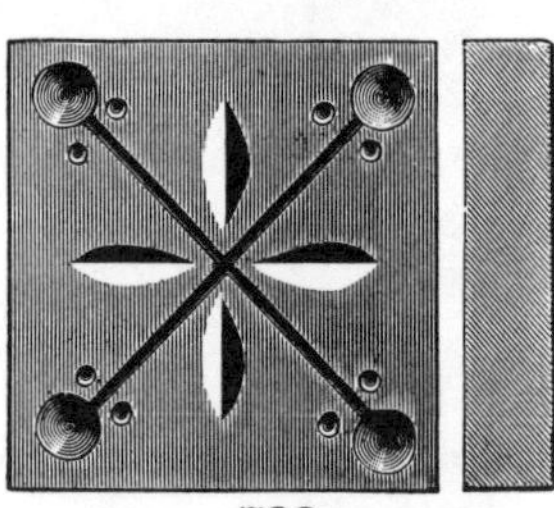

792

5 to 6 in. sq. × 1⅛ $7.00 per 100

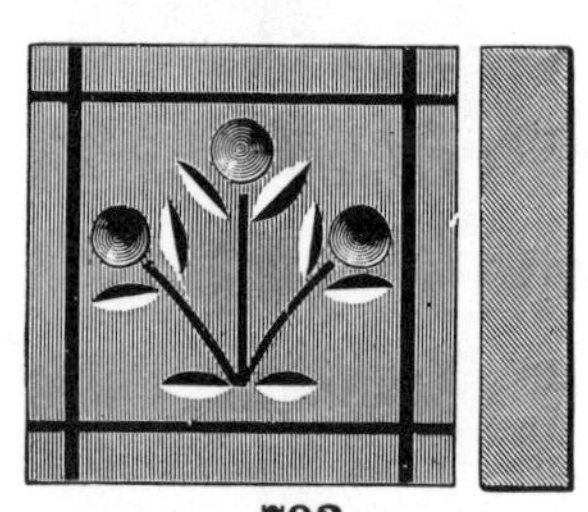

793

5 to 6 in. sq. × 1⅛ $7.00 per 100

794

5 to 6 in. sq. × 1⅛ $6.50 per 100

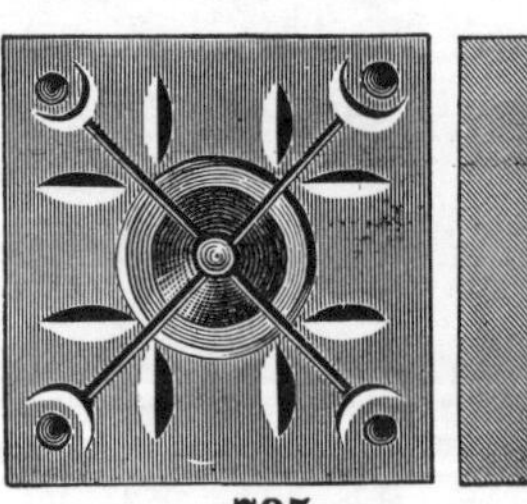

795

5 to 6 in. sq. × 1⅛ $7.50 per 100

796

5 to 6 in. sq. × 1⅛ $6.00 per 100

WOOD CORNER BLOCKS.

798—A
5⅜ inches square, $42.00 per 100

798—B
5⅜ and 5¾ inches square, $42.00 per 100

798—C
5⅜ and 5¾ inches square, $42.00 per 100

798—D
5⅜ and 5¾ inches square, $42.00 per 100

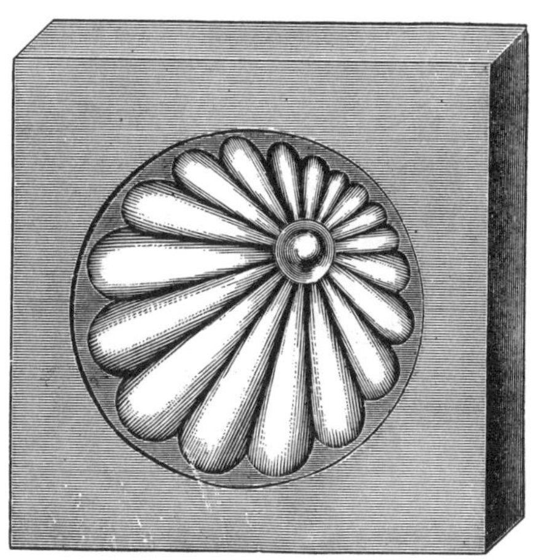

798—E
5⅜ and 5¾ inches square, $42.00 per 100

798—F
5⅜ and 5¾ inches square, $42.00 per 100

WOOD HEAD BLOCKS.

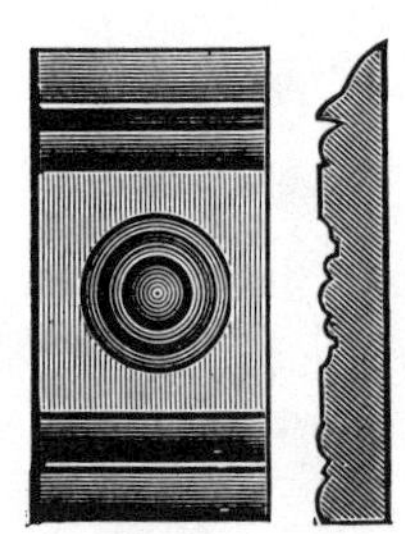

802

5½×10, $10.00 per 100

803

5½×10, $18.00 per 100

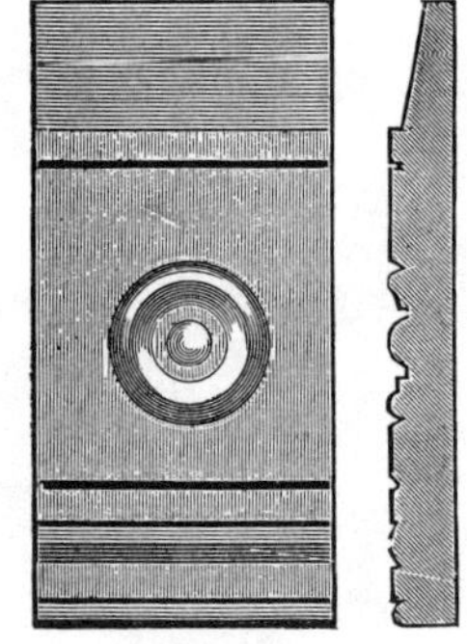

804

5½×10, $10.00 per 100

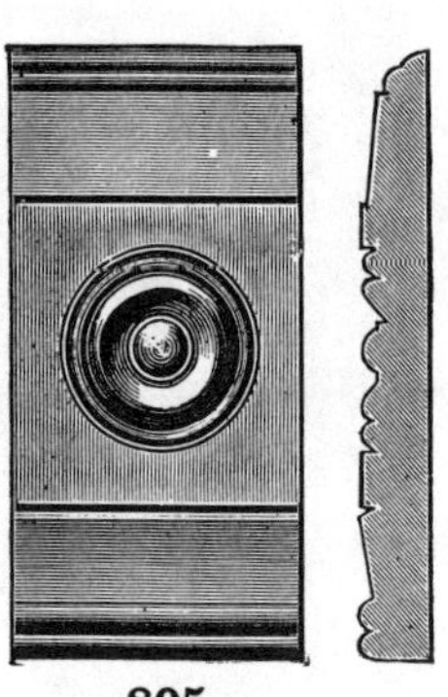

805

5½×10, $11.00 per 100

806

5½×11, $15.00 per 100

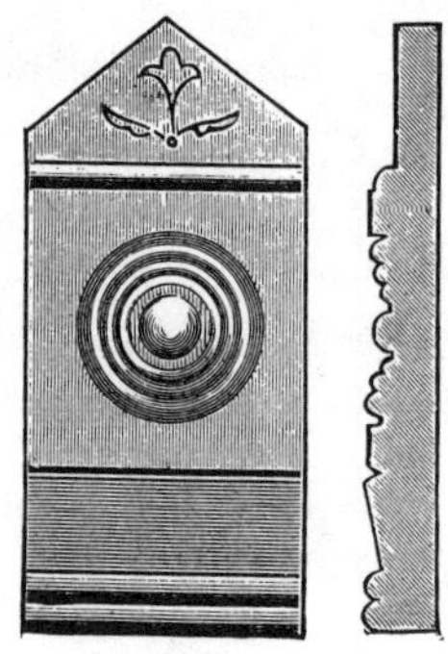

807

5½×11, $16.00 per 100

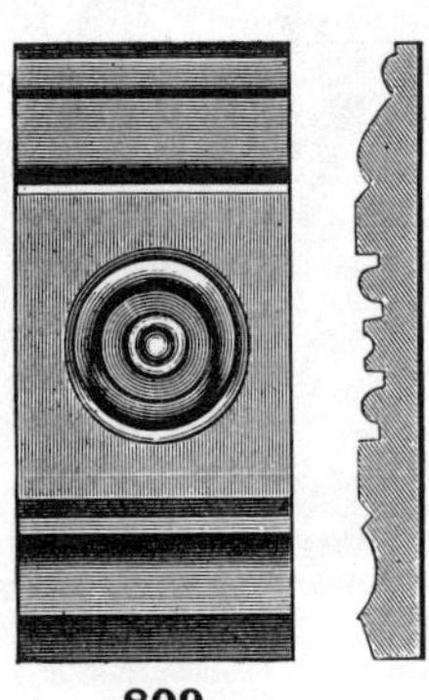

809

5½×10, $10.00 per 100

810

5½×10, $10.00 per 100

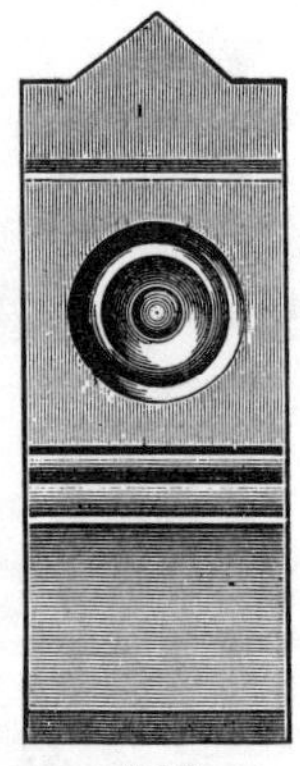

811

5½×12, $14.00 per 100

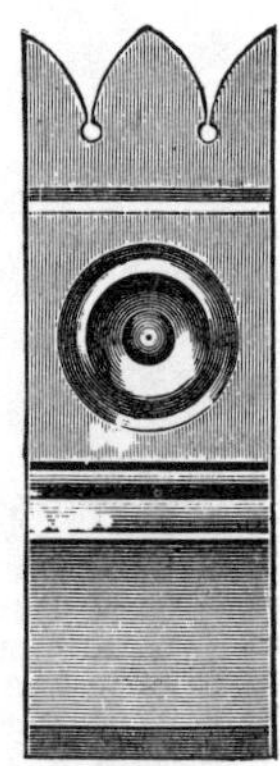

812

5½×12, $16.00 per 100

Above Blocks are 1⅛ inches thick.

WOOD HEAD BLOCKS.

814
5½×11, $13.00 per 100

815
5½×11, $11.00 per 100

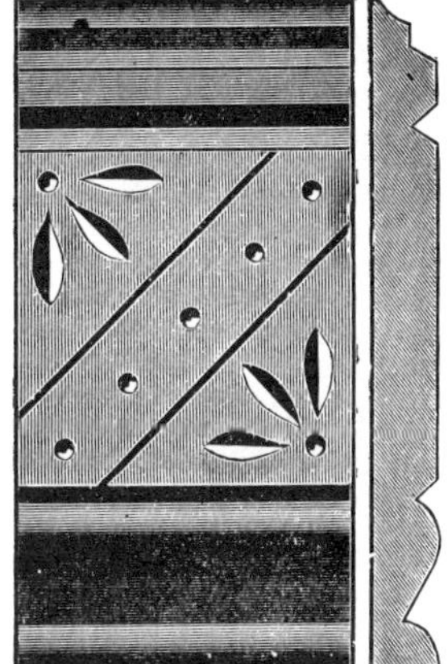

816
5½×11, $11.00 per 100

817
5½×10, $12.00 per 100

818
5½×10, $11.00 per 100

819
5½×12, $12.00 per 100

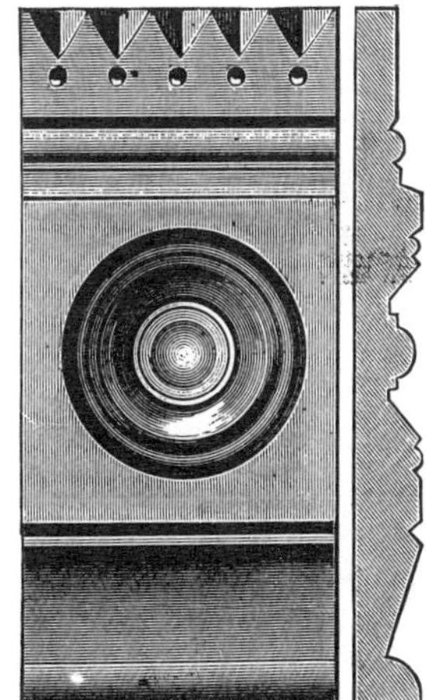

820
5½×12, $15.00 per 100

821
5½×9½, $12.00 per 100

822
5½×10, $30.00 per 100

Above Blocks are 1⅛ inches thick.

WOOD HEAD BLOCKS.

823

5½ × 10, $17.00 per 100

824

5½ × 10, $12.00 per 100

825

5½ × 11, hand carved, $120.00 per 100

825—A

3 inches Square, $16.00 per 100

825—B

3½ inches Square, $17.00 per 100

825—C

3 inches Square, $17.00 per 100

825—A, B, and C are Pressed Wood Ornaments, which can be used for center pieces of Corner or Head Blocks, at greatly reduced price over hand carving, and equally as effective.

826

5½ × 10, $12.00 per 100

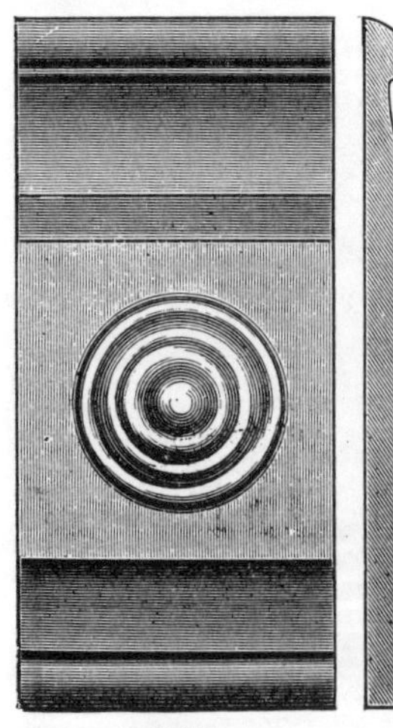

827

5½ × 10½, $11.00 per 100

828

5½ × 10, $11.00 per 100

WOOD HEAD BLOCKS.

829

5½ × 10½ × 1⅛, $30.00 per 100

830

5½ × 11 × 1⅛, $20.00 per 100

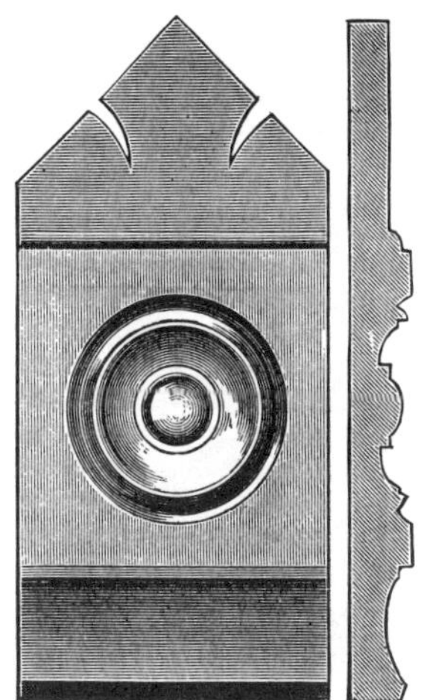

831

5½ × 10½ × 1⅛, $14.00 per 100

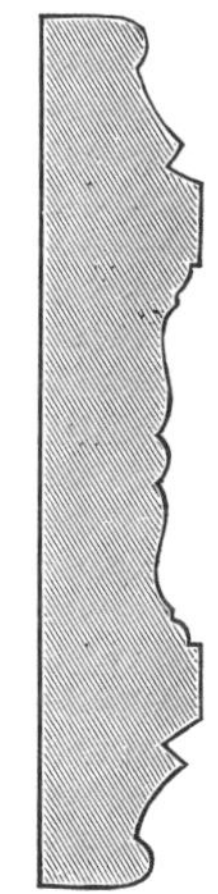

832

5 to 5¾ × 9 × 1⅜ thick, $40.00
6 to 6¾ × 10 × 1⅜ " 45.00

833

5 to 5¾ × 13 × 1⅜ thick, $50.00
6 to 6¾ × 13 × 1⅜ " 60.00
7 to 8 × 13 × 1⅜ " 75.00

832–A

2½ in. Square, $9.00 per 100

Can be used as Center for
Head Blocks.

WOOD HEAD BLOCKS.

834

5½ × 12½, $60.00 per 100

835

5½ × 11½, $13 00 per 100

836

5½ × 12, $24 00 per 100

836—A

836—B

836—C

836—A, B, and C are Wood Ornaments, which can be used with good effect for centers of Corners and Head Blocks.

837

5½ × 12, $50.00 per 100

839

5½ × 12½, $25.00 per 100

844

5½ × 12, $55.00 per 100

WOOD BASE OR PLINTH BLOCKS.

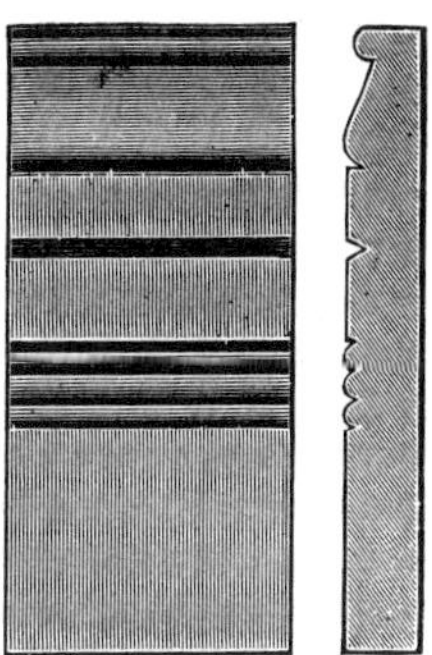

900

5½ × 10 × 1⅜, $11.00 per 100

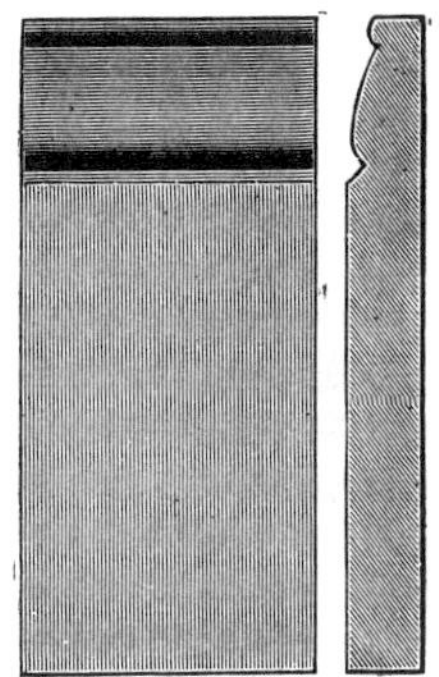

901

5½ × 9 × 1⅜, $8.00 per 100

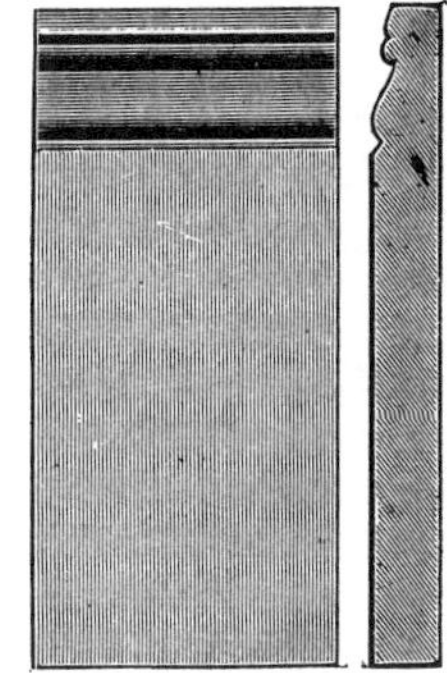

902

5½ × 9 × 1⅜, $9.00 per 100

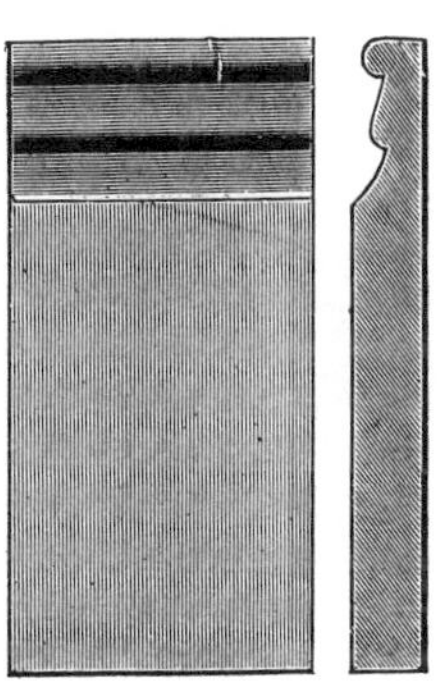

903

5½ × 8 × 1⅜, $8.00 per 100

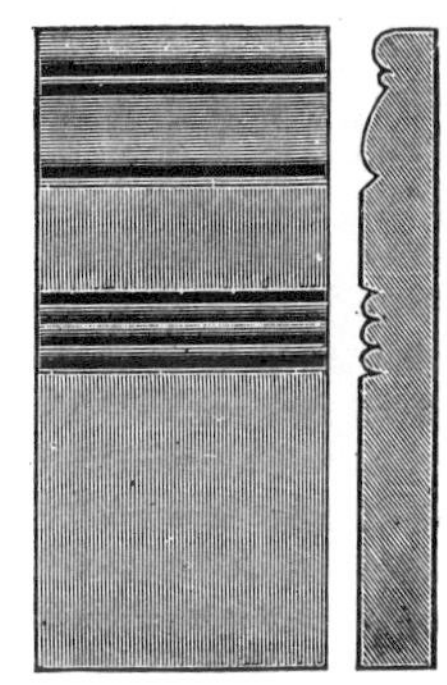

904

5½ × 10 × 1⅜, $11.00 per 100

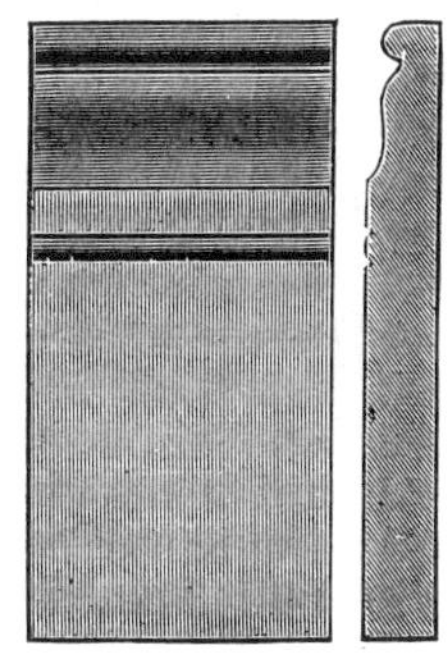

905

5½ × 10 × 1⅜, $9 00 per 100

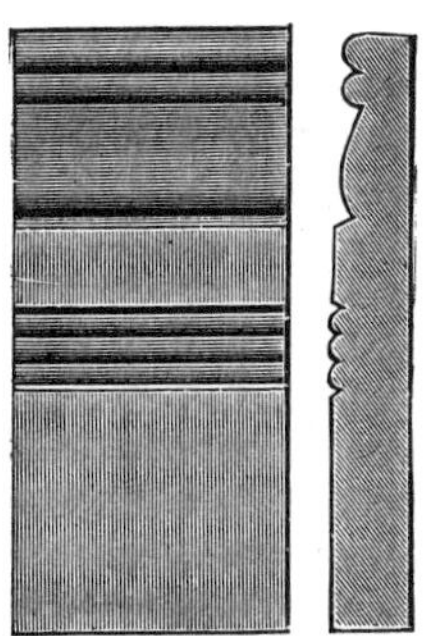

906

5½ × 10 × 1⅜, $11.00 per 100

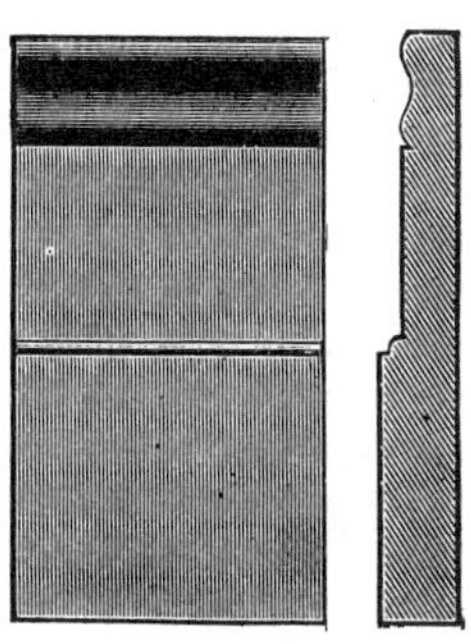

907

5½ × 10 × 1⅜, $10.00 per 100

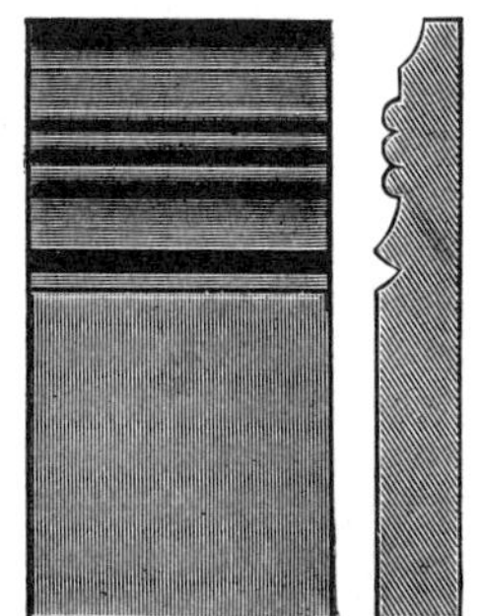

908

5½ × 10 × 1⅜, $10.00 per 100

WOOD BASE OR PLINTH BLOCKS.

909

5½ × 12 × 1⅜, $12.00 per 100

910

5½ × 10 × 1⅜, $10.00 per 100

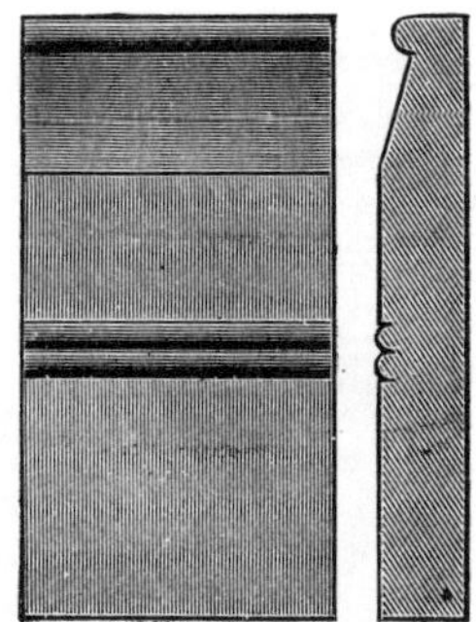

911

5½ × 10 × 1⅜, $10.00 per 100

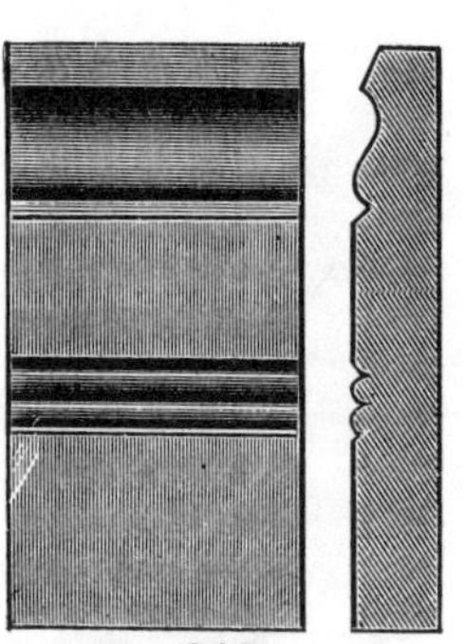

912

5½ × 10 × 1⅜, $10.00 per 100

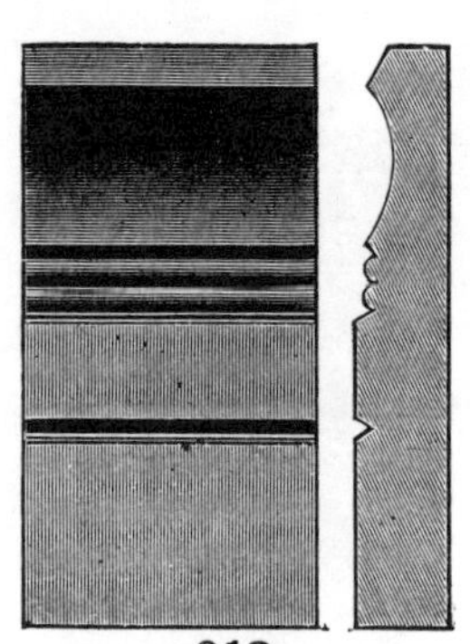

913

5½ × 10 × 1⅜, $11.00 per 100

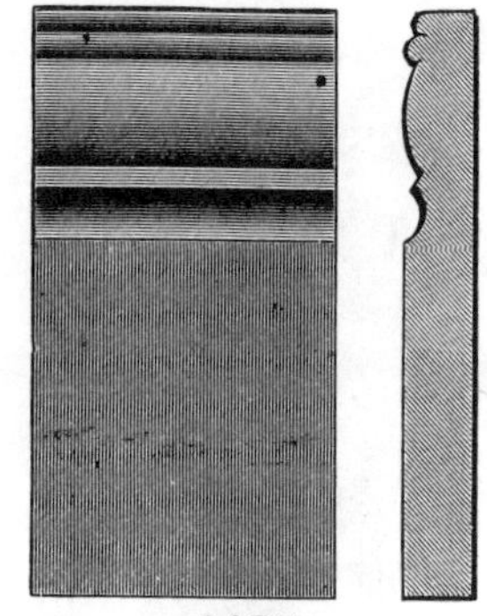

913½

5½ × 10 × 1⅜, $9.50 per 100

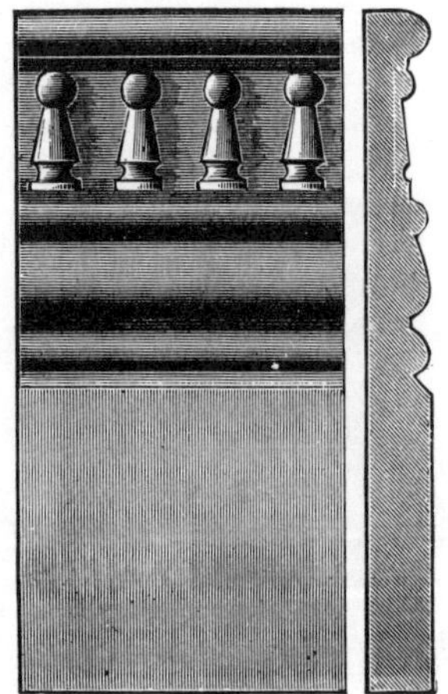

914

5½ × 12 × 1⅜, $20.00 per 100

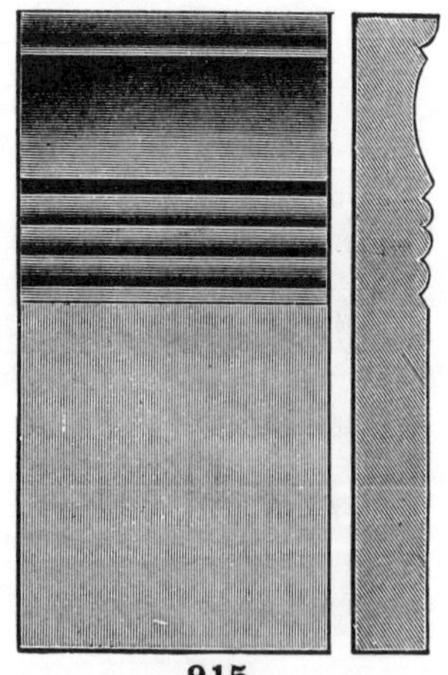

915

5½ × 11 × 1⅜, $11.00 per 100

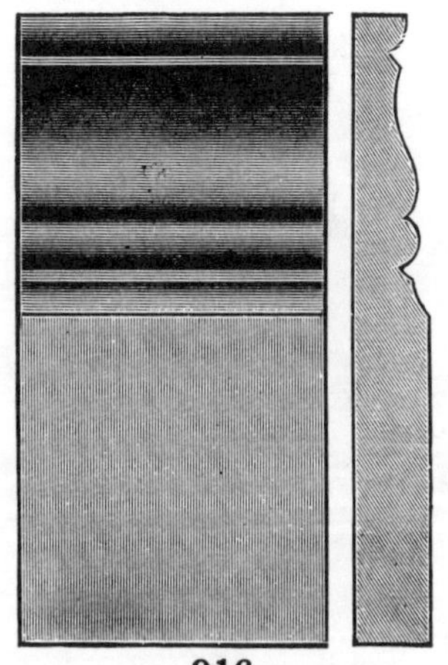

916

5½ × 11 × 1⅜, $11.00 per 100

WOOD BASE OR PLINTH BLOCKS.

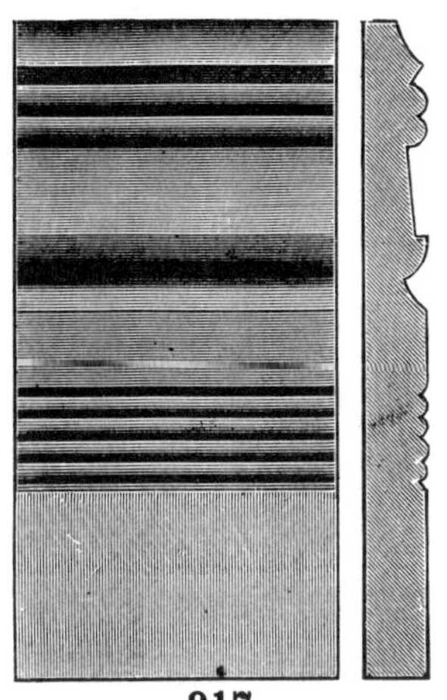

917

5½×11×1⅜, $13.00 per 100

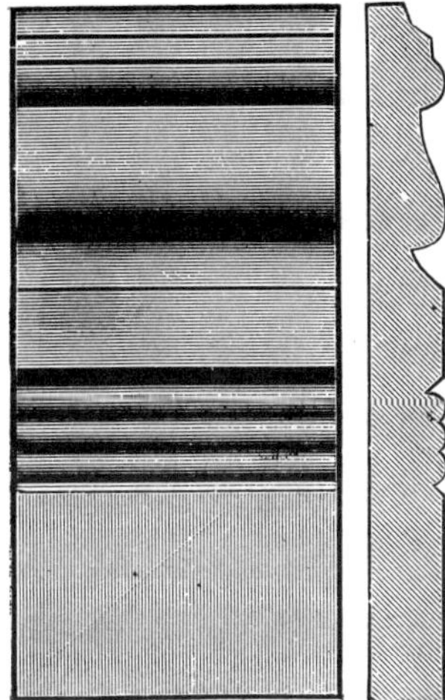

918

5½×12×1⅜, $13.00 per 100

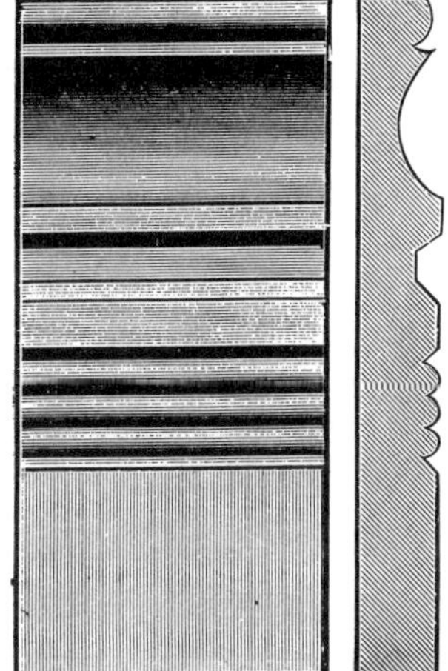

929

5½×12×1⅜, $13.00 per 100

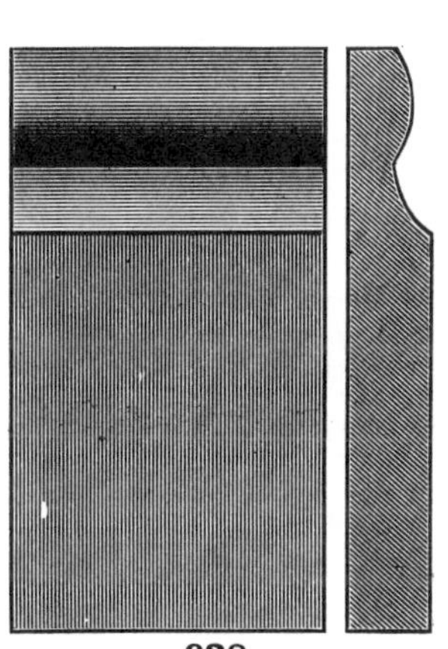

938

5½×10×1⅜, $8.00 per 100

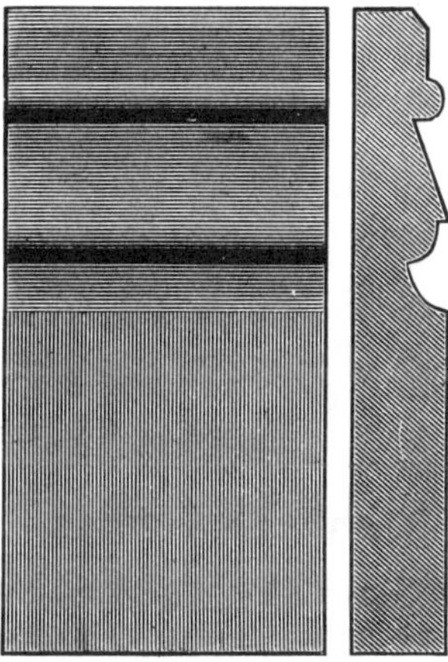

940

5½×11×1⅜, $9.50 per 100

941

5½×10×1⅜, $8.00 per 100

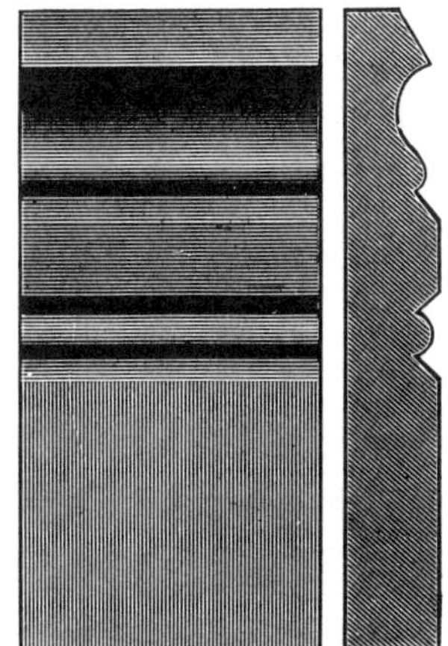

944

5½×11×1⅜, $9.00 per 100

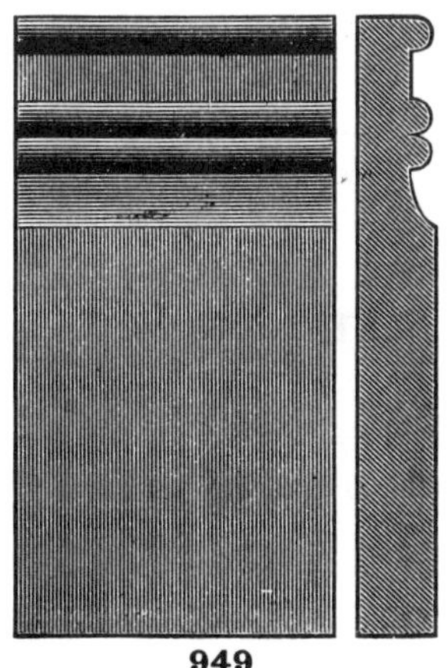

949

5½×10×1⅜, $8.00 per 100

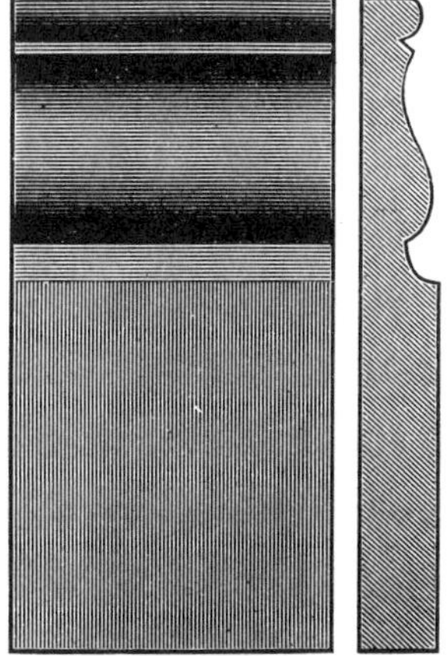

950

5½×12×1⅜, $9.50 per 100

Hardwood Mantels.

ON PAGES 89 TO 110, INCLUSIVE, ARE SHOWN A FEW DESIGNS THAT HAVE BEEN SELECTED AS MEETING THE POPULAR DEMAND.

SIZE. Stock size of all Mantels is 5 feet, but Mantels can be widened to 5 feet 6 inches by extending the wall plates. We will always widen Mantels in this way unless otherwise specified. If Mantel is wider than 5 feet 6 inches, or narrower than 5 feet, an extra price will be charged.

WOOD. Mantels marked made only in Red Oak or Birch, are manufactured in large quantities in these two woods, and carried in stock, consequently we are enabled to list them at a very low price. They will be made to order in other woods, if desired, at special prices. All other designs are made in any of the native hardwoods (see below).

TILES. Enameled and Embossed Tiles come in nearly every shade and tint. Where colors of tiling are not specified, we always select those which harmonize best with the wood of the Mantel.

TRIMMINGS. We can furnish Brass and Wrought Iron goods, Andirons, Fenders, Fire Sets, Frames, Grates, and Portable Baskets, Iron Linings, etc., and can ship any of these goods with Mantels.

PRICES. We have made our prices in a way that will enable any one to arrange the Mantel they may select, with any of the trimmings shown in catalogue. Everything that is necessary to set the Mantel, just as shown in cut, is included, except **75** common brick and a little mortar. We name each article that we include.

In ordering, state width of chimney-breast, and kind of wood and finish wanted.

NATIVE WOODS.

Red Oak, natural or antique.
Birch, natural or stained mahogany.
Cherry, natural or antique.
Quarter-Sawed White Oak, natural or antique.
Quarter-Sawed Sycamore.
Gum Wood.
Ash, natural or antique.
Walnut.
California Red Wood.
White Maple.
Butternut.
Sixteenth Century Finish, Cremona Finish, and Old English Oak.

EXTRA WOODS.

Mahogany, natural or antique.
Prima Vera.
Bird's-Eye Maple.
Curly Birch.
White and Gold.

MANTELS.

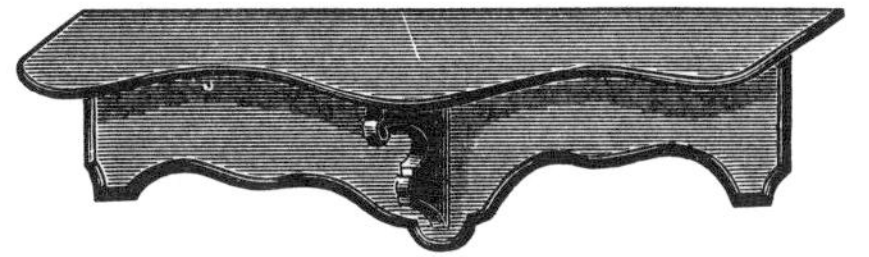

2100

From 18 to 30 inches long.

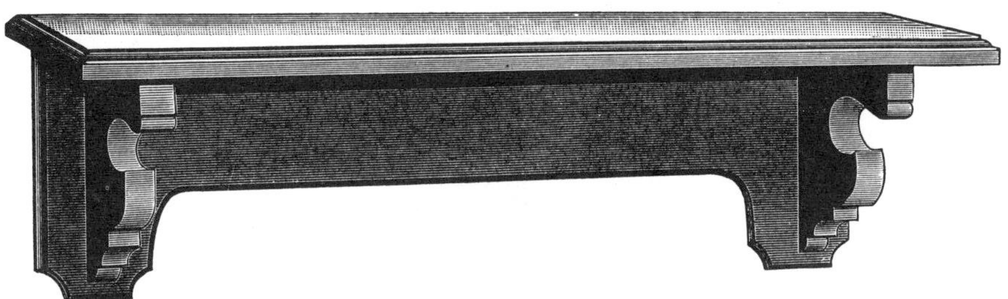

2101

2102

WRITE FOR PRICES.

MANTELS.

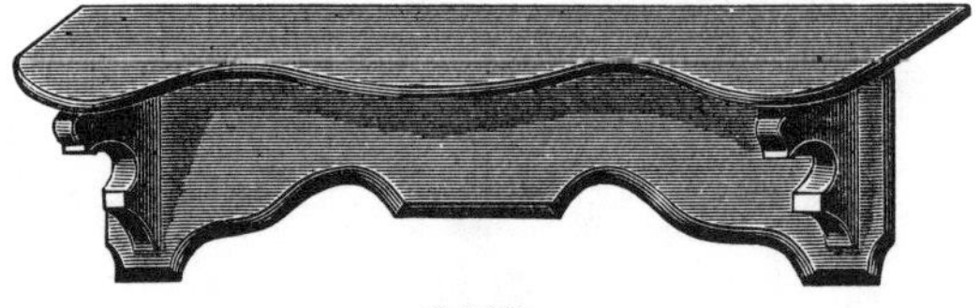

2103

From 30 to 48 inches long.

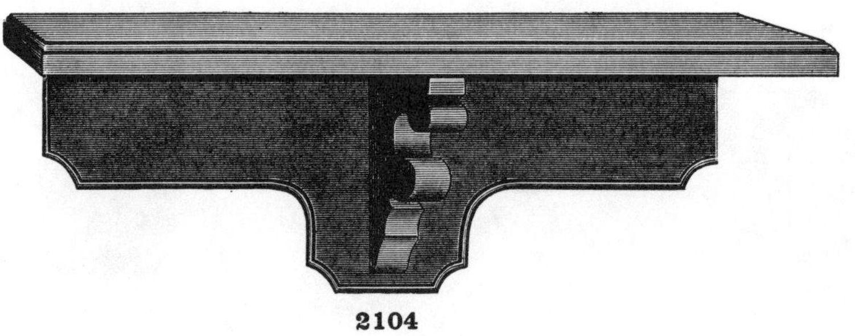

2104

2105

WRITE FOR PRICES.

MANTELS.

2106

2107

WRITE FOR PRICES.

MANTELS.

2108

2109

MANTEL.

2110

MANTEL.

2111

MANTEL.

2112

MANTEL.

2113

MANTEL.

2114

MANTEL.

2115

MANTEL.

2116

MANTEL.

2117

MANTEL.

2118

MANTEL.

2119

Length of Shelf... 5 feet.
Width of Opening .... 2 " 11½ inches.
Width of Opening may be varied up to.......................... 3 " 6 "
Height of Opening... 2 " 11¾ "
Profile .... 4 "
Height of Mantel from floor to highest point .... 6 " 5 "
Size of Mirror .... 40 x 18 "
 If length of Shelf is increased, the size and cost of Mirror will be increased proportionately.

WRITE FOR PRICES.

MANTEL.

2120

Length of Shelf.. 5 feet.
Width of Opening .... 2 " 11½ inches.
Width of Opening may be varied up to................................ 3 "   6   "
Height of Opening... 2 " 11¾ "
Profile   7   "
Height of Mantel from floor to highest point .... 6 "
Size of Mirror ....   40 x 12 "
 If length of Shelf is increased, the size and cost of Mirror will be increased proportionately.

WRITE FOR PRICES.

MANTEL.

2121

Length of Shelf .... 5 feet.
Width of Opening .... 2 " 11½ inches.
Width of Opening may be varied up to .... 3 " 6   "
Height of Opening .... 2 " 11¾ "
Profile 8   "
Height of Mantel from floor to highest point .... 6 " 8   "
Size of Mirror .... 28 x 20   "

If length of Shelf is increased, the size and cost of Mirror will be increased proportionately.

WRITE FOR PRICES.

MANTEL.

2122

Length of Shelf... 5 feet.
Width of Opening... 2 " 11½ inches.
    Width of Opening can not be increased without increasing length of Shelf.
Height of Opening.. 2 " 11¾ "
Profile.. 7 "
Height of Mantel from floor to highest point............................... 6 ' 5 "
Size of Mirror... 28 x 20 "

WRITE FOR PRICES.

MANTEL.

2123

Length of Shelf... 5 feet.
Width of Opening .... 2 " 11¼ inches.
Height of Opening... 2 " 11¼ "
By moving back Side Linings, width of Opening may be varied up to........... 3 " 6 "

WRITE FOR PRICES.

MANTEL.

2124

Length of Shelf.. 5 feet.

Width of Opening .... 2 " 11½ inches.

Height of Opening.. 2 " 11¾ "

WRITE FOR PRICES.

MANTEL.

2125

Length of Shelf.. 5 feet.
Width of Opening .... 2 " 11½ inches.
Height of Opening.. 2 " 11¾ "

WRITE FOR PRICES.

MANTEL.

2126

Length of Shelf.. 5 feet.
Width of Opening.. 2 " 11½ inches.
Height of Opening.. 2 " 11¾ "

MANTEL.

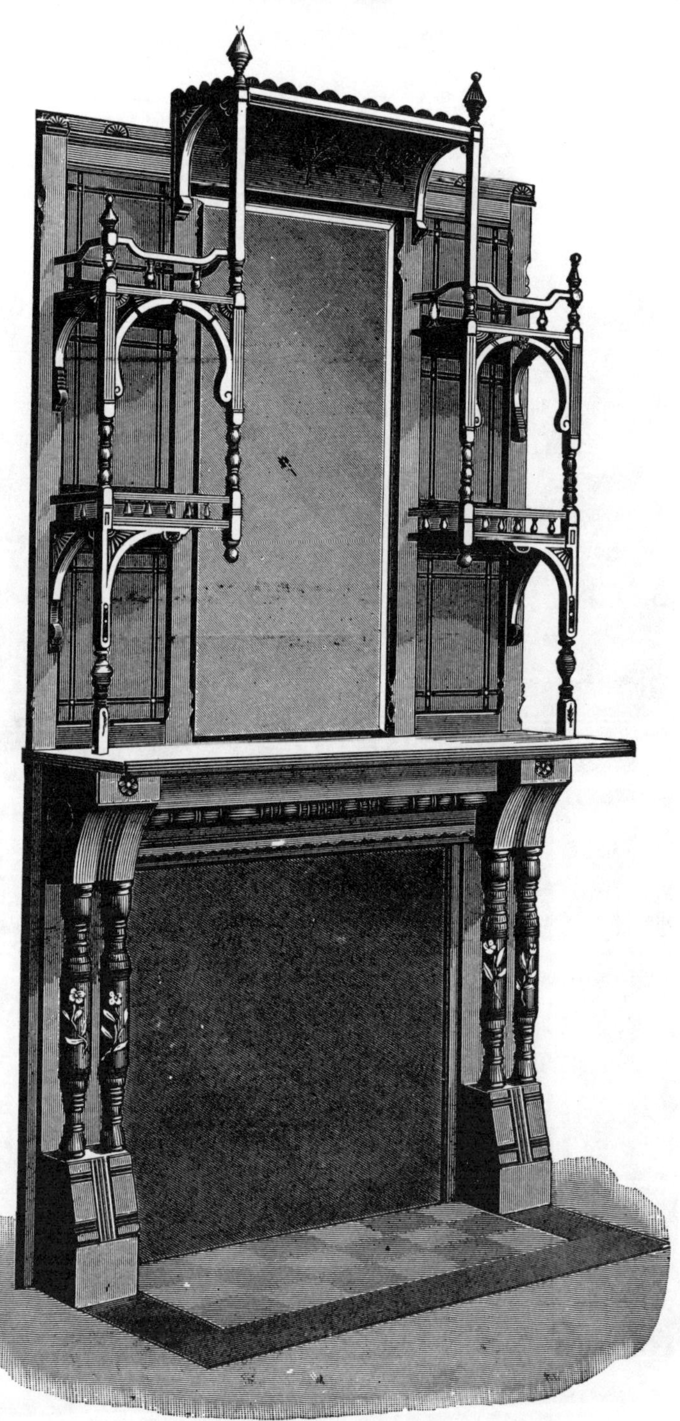

2127

Length of Shelf .... 5 feet.
Width of Opening.. 2 " 11½ inches.
Height of Opening.. 2 " 11¾ "
By moving back Side Linings, width of Opening may be varied up to..... ...... 3 " 6 "

WRITE FOR PRICES.

OFFICE AND BANK COUNTERS.

2200

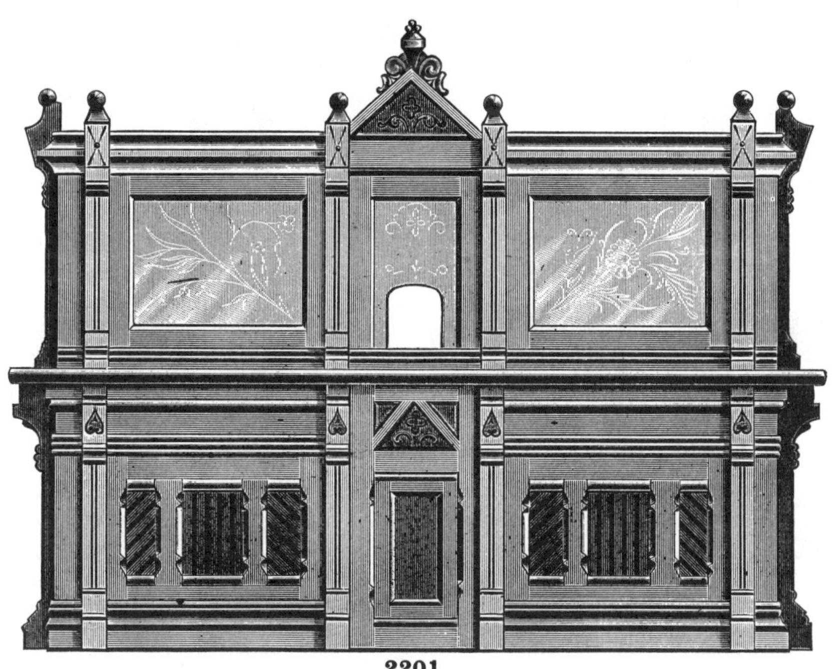

2201

PULPITS.

2225

2226

2227

2228

2232

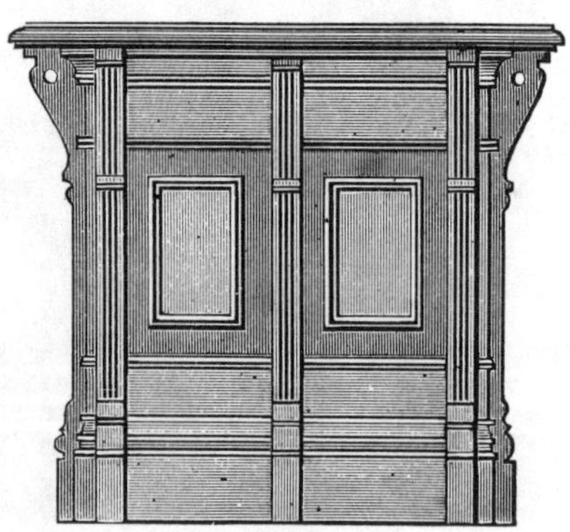

2233

WRITE FOR PRICES.

PEW ENDS.

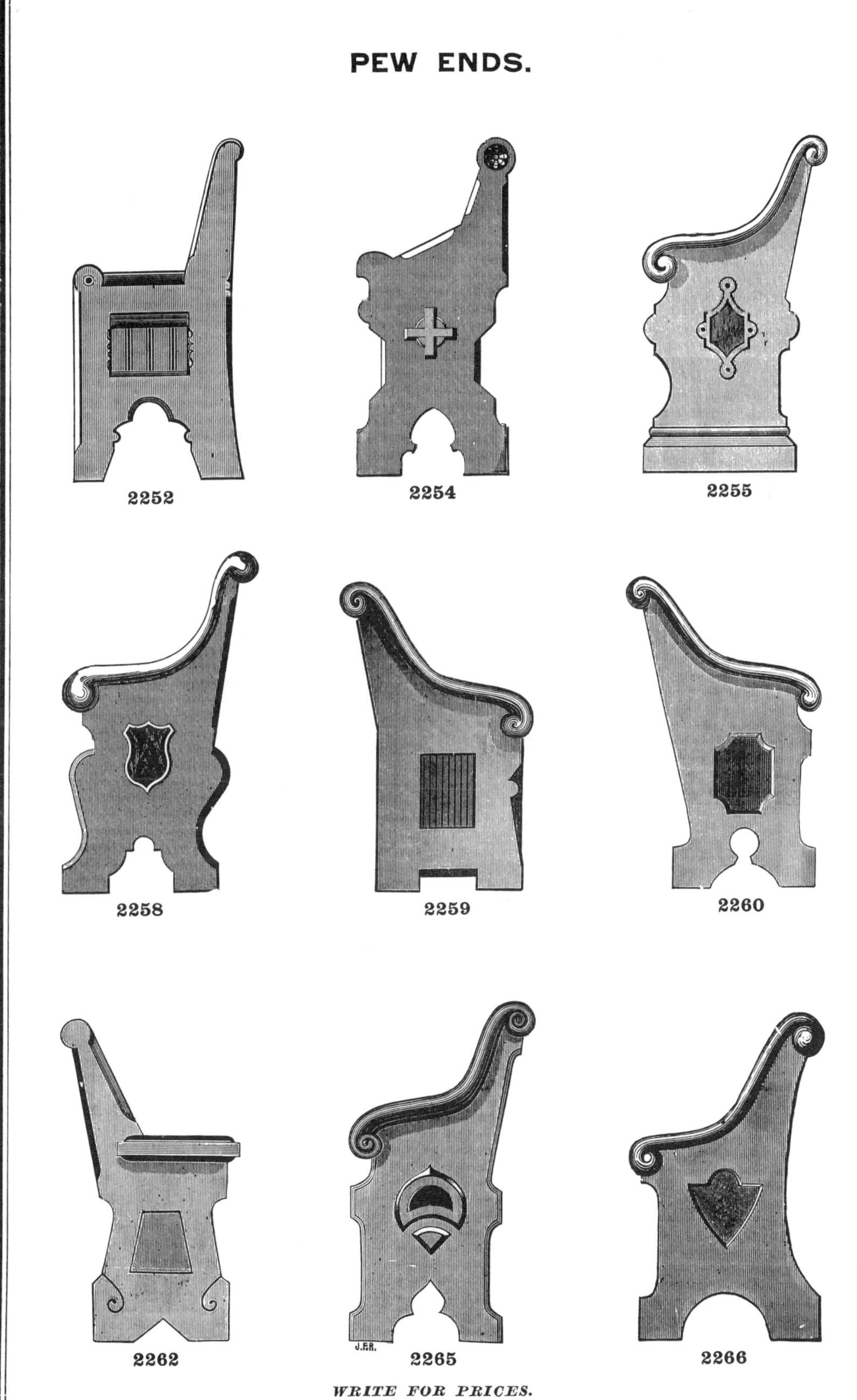

2252

2254

2255

2258

2259

2260

2262

2265

2266

WRITE FOR PRICES.

Interior Hardwood Finish.

WE would especially call your attention to our revised list of the latest styles of Mouldings, as shown on pages Nos. 115 to 136 inclusive. We make a specialty of furnishing these, in any kind of hardwood, either in large or small quantities. Also, if you should fancy a design from some other catalogue, by sending sketch or detail of same, it will be furnished you as cheerfully as if selected from our catalogue, and at as reasonable prices.

Any information in assisting you in ordering your goods in conformity to our designs, and to apply to your particular work, will be cheerfully sent you on application.

Yours respectfully,

BLUMER & KUHN STAIR CO.

CASINGS.

497
13–16 × 5⅜
498
13–16 × 5⅜
499
13–16 × 5⅜
500
13–16 × 5⅜
501
13–16 × 5⅜
502
13–16 × 5⅜

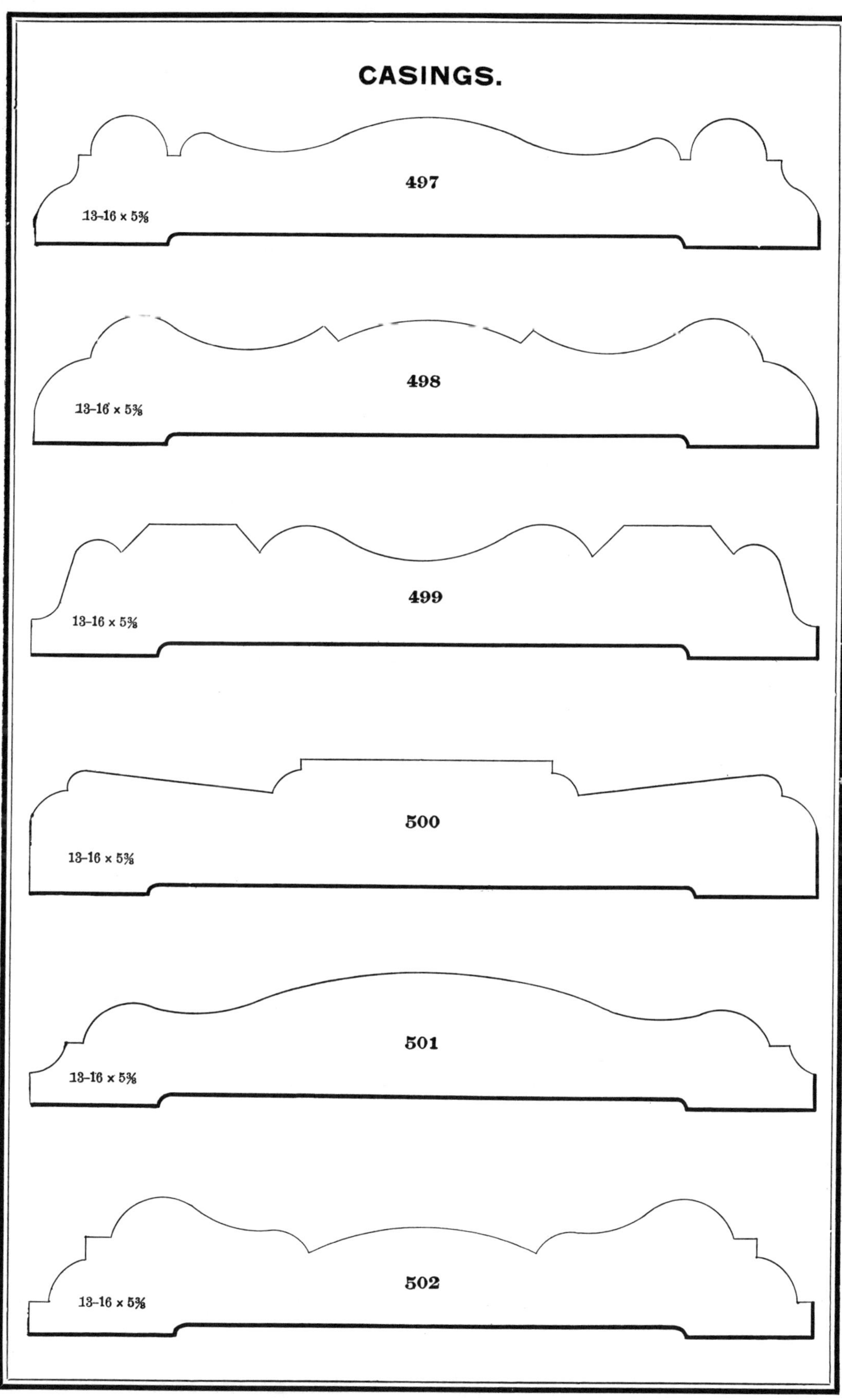

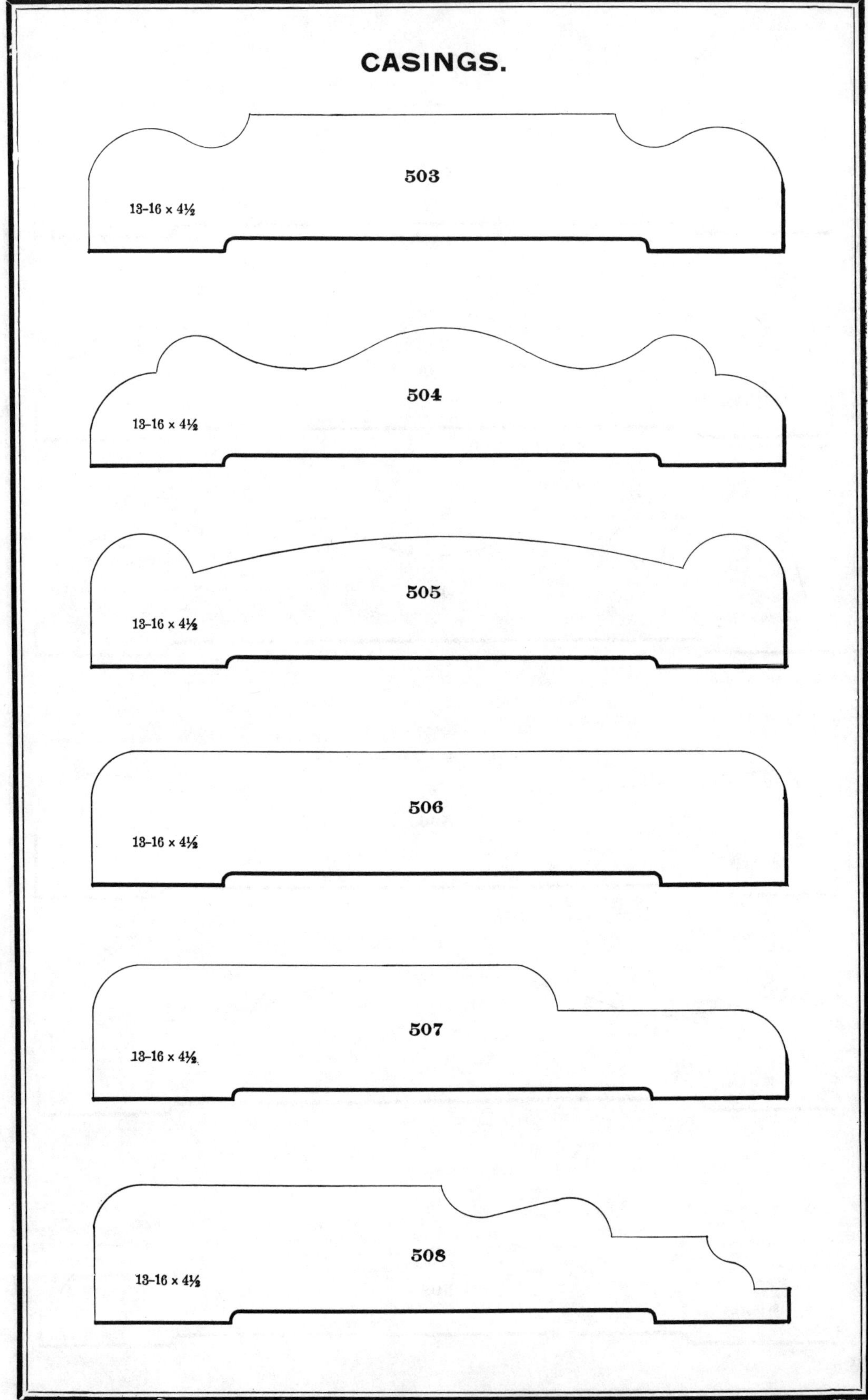
CASINGS.
503
13–16 x 4½
504
13–16 x 4½
505
13–16 x 4½
506
13–16 x 4½
507
13–16 x 4½
508
13–16 x 4½

EASTLAKE AND QUEEN ANNE CASINGS.

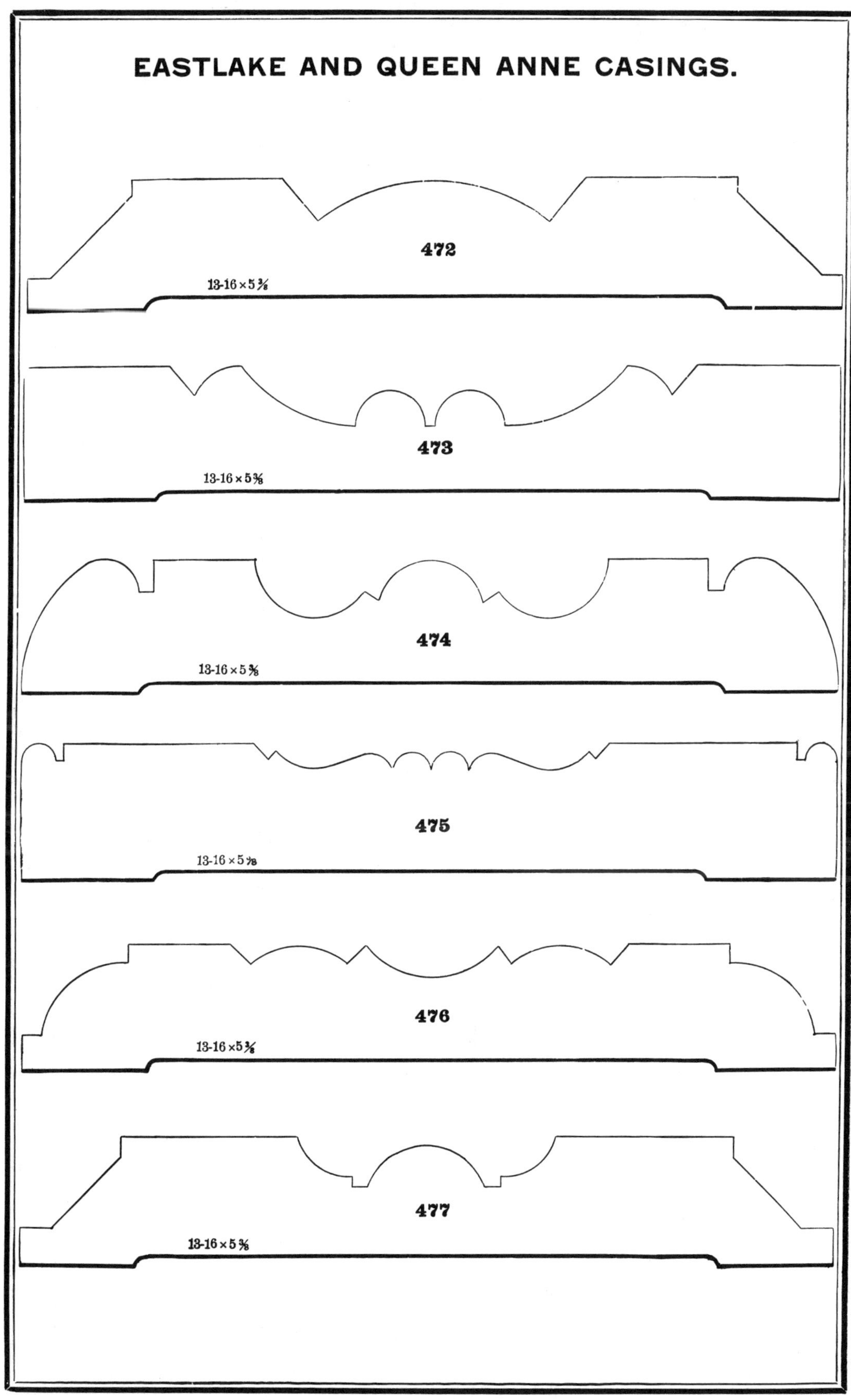

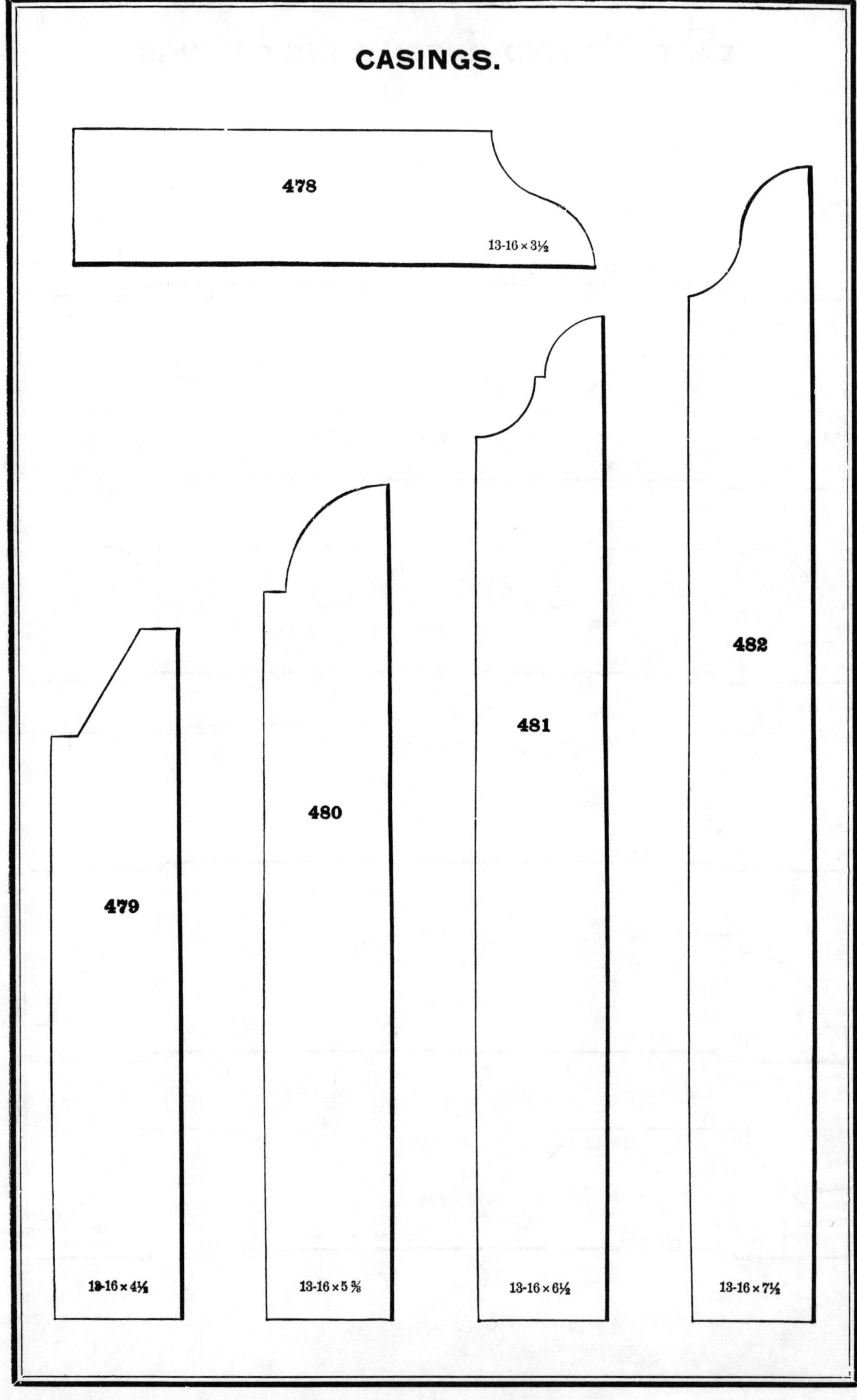

CASINGS.
478
13-16 × 3½
479
480
481
482
13-16 × 4½
13-16 × 5 ⅜
13-16 × 6½
13-16 × 7½

CASINGS.

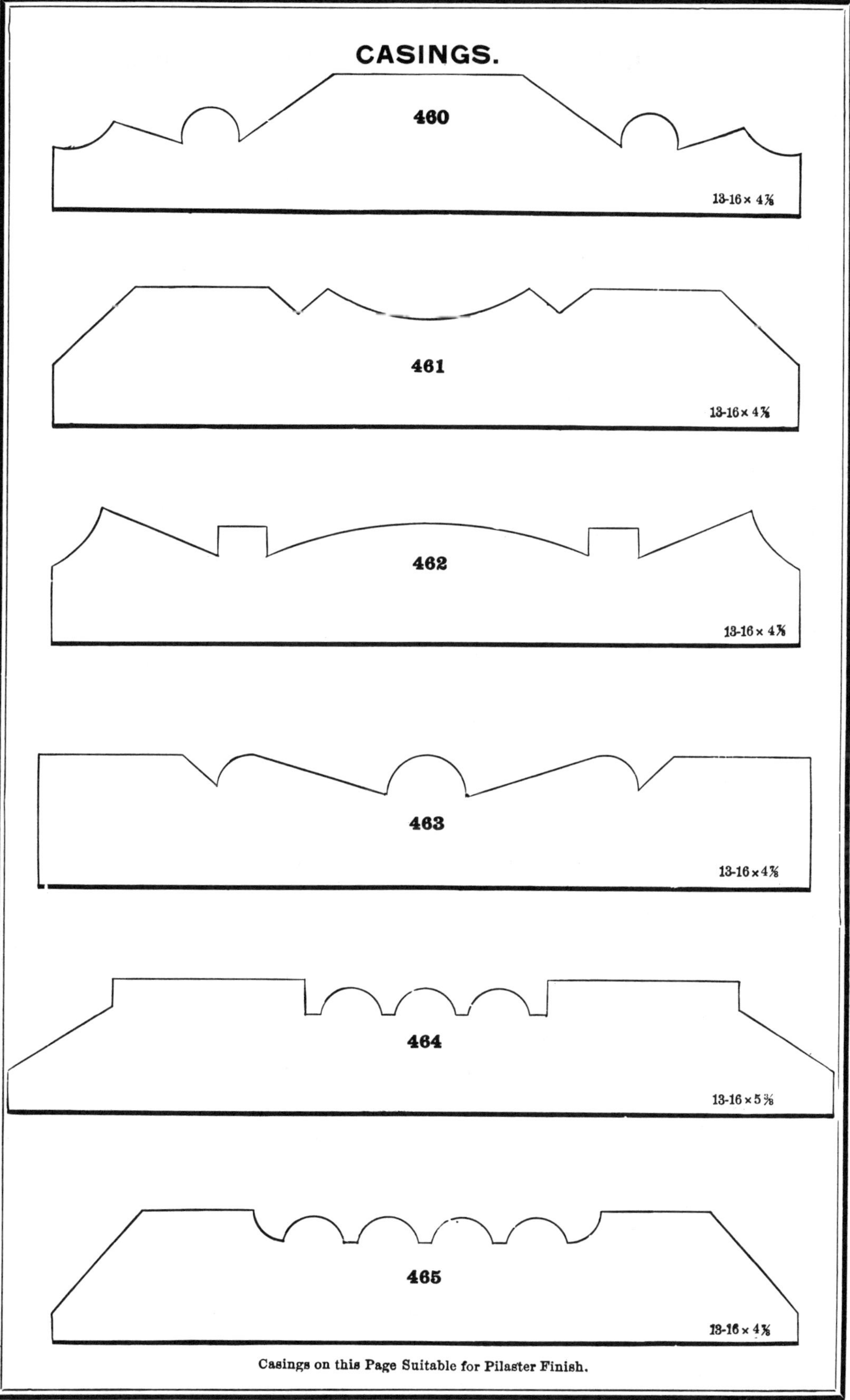

Casings on this Page Suitable for Pilaster Finish.

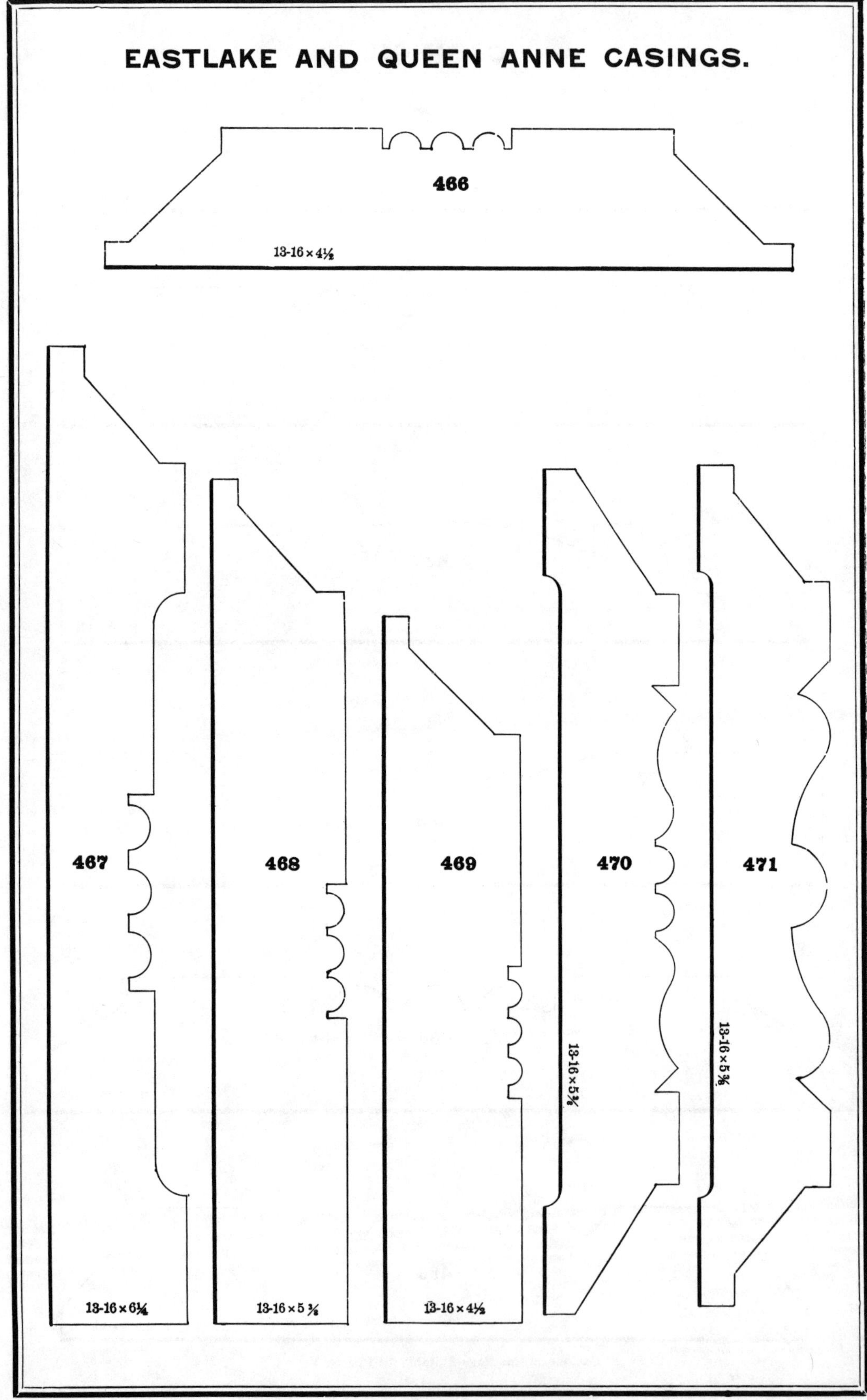

EASTLAKE AND QUEEN ANNE CASINGS.
466
13-16 × 4½
467
468
469
470
471
13-16 × 6¼
13-16 × 5 ⅜
13-16 × 4½
13-16 × 5⅝
13-16 × 5⅝

CASINGS.

509
13–16 x 4⅞
510
13–16 x 4⅞
511
13–16 x 4⅞
512
13–16 x 4⅞
513
13–16 x 4⅞
514
13–16 x 4⅞

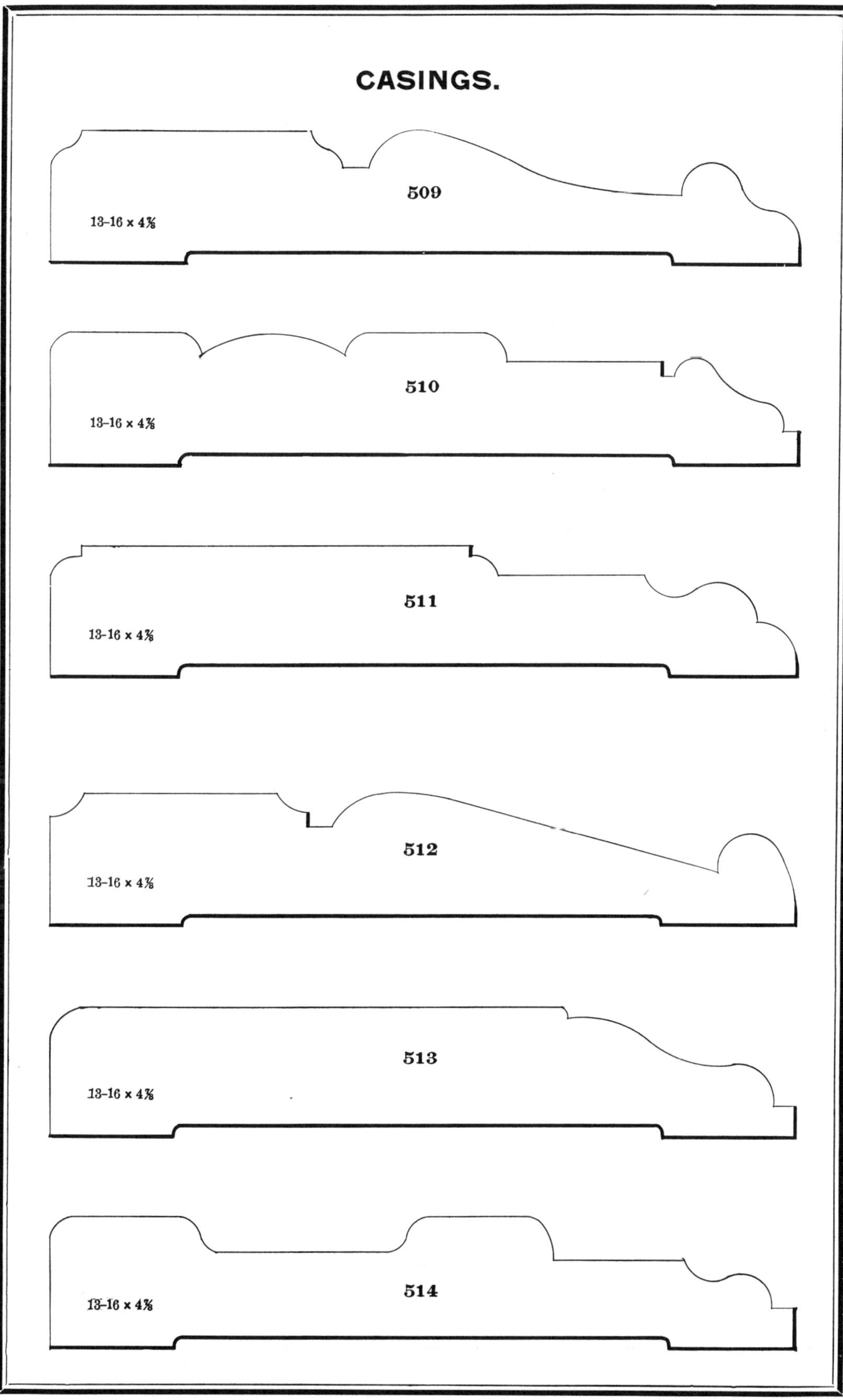

INSIDE FINISH.

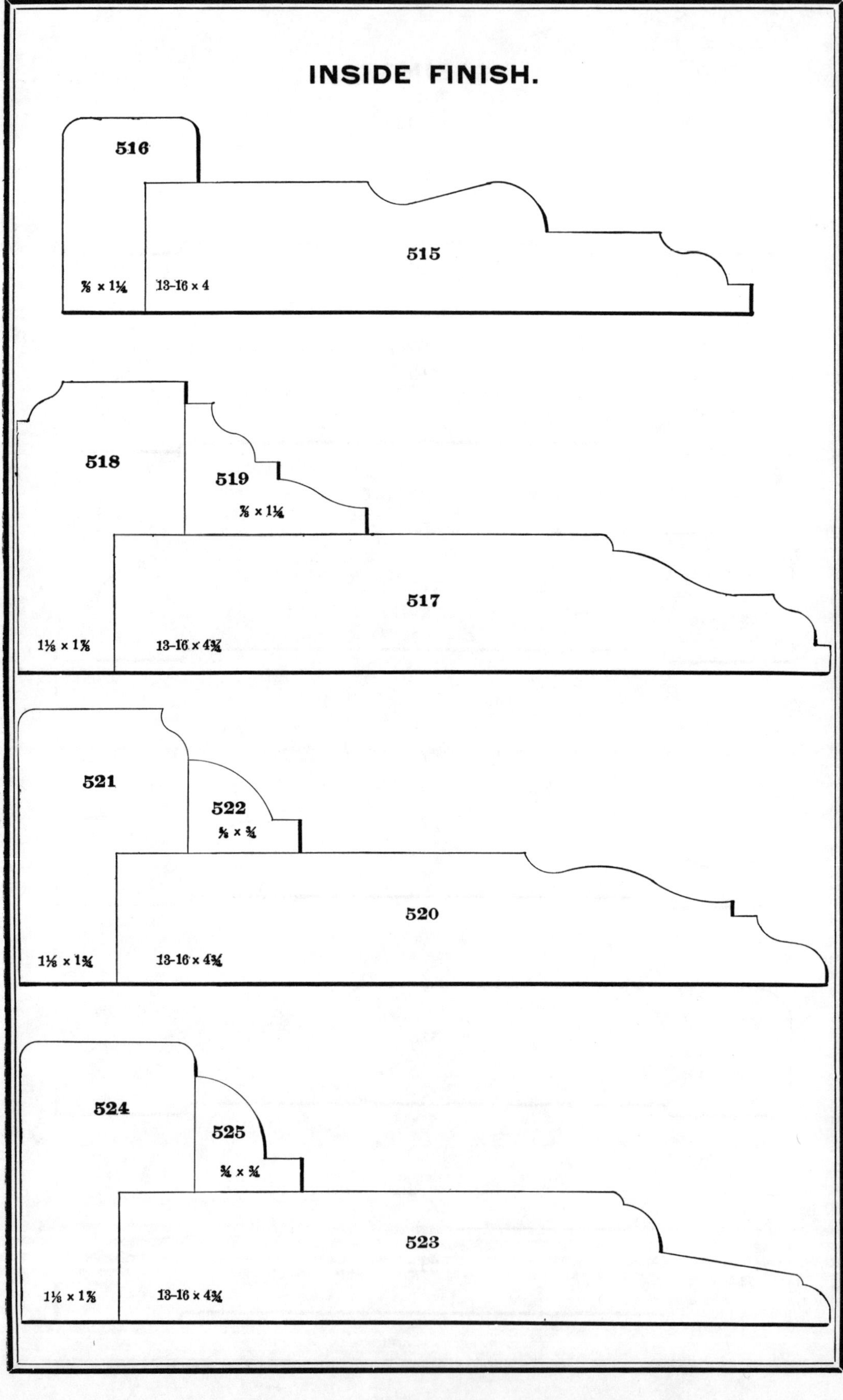

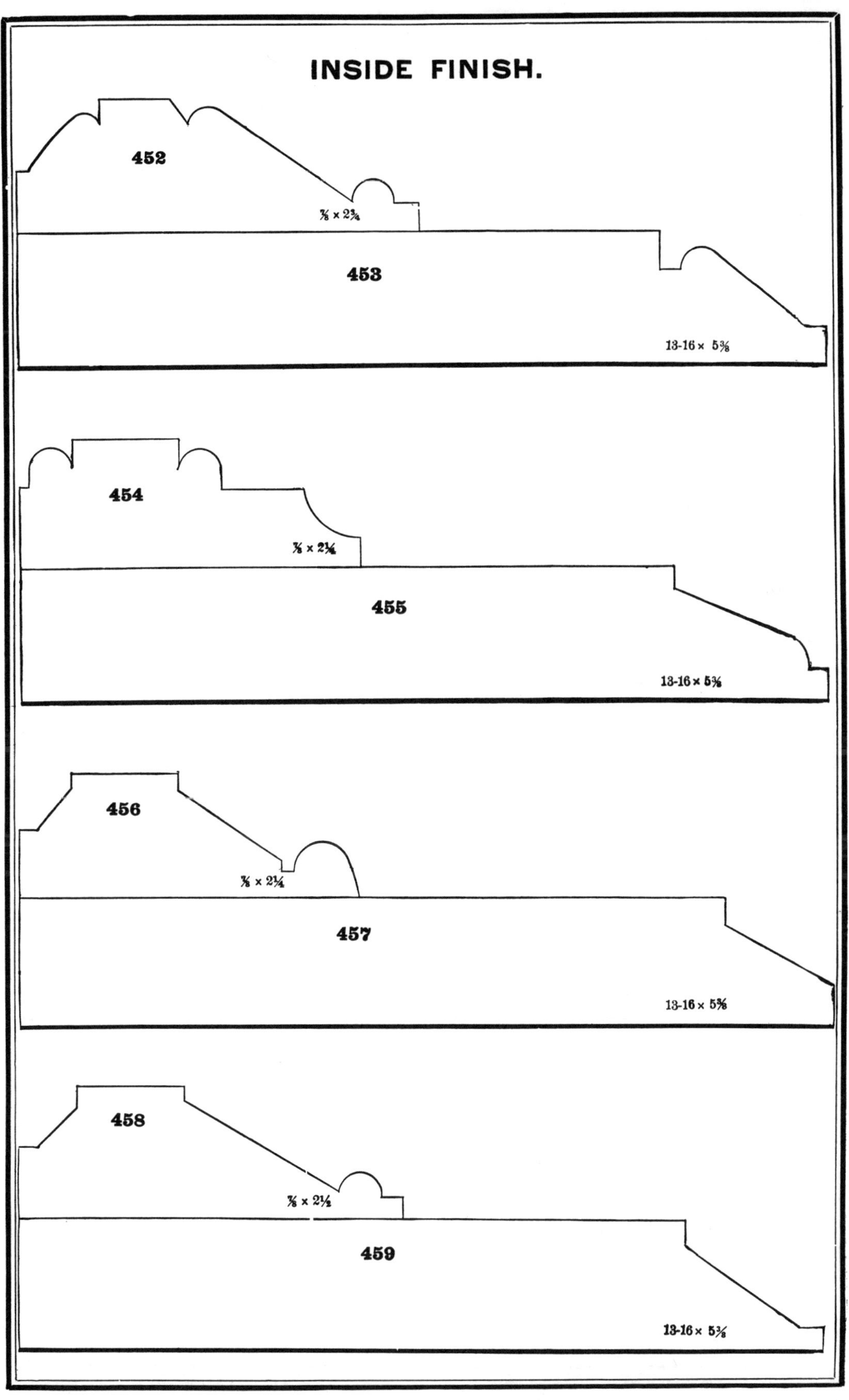
INSIDE FINISH.
452
⅞ × 2¾
453
13-16 × 5⅜
454
⅞ × 2¼
455
13-16 × 5⅜
456
⅞ × 2¼
457
13-16 × 5⅜
458
⅞ × 2½
459
13-16 × 5⅜

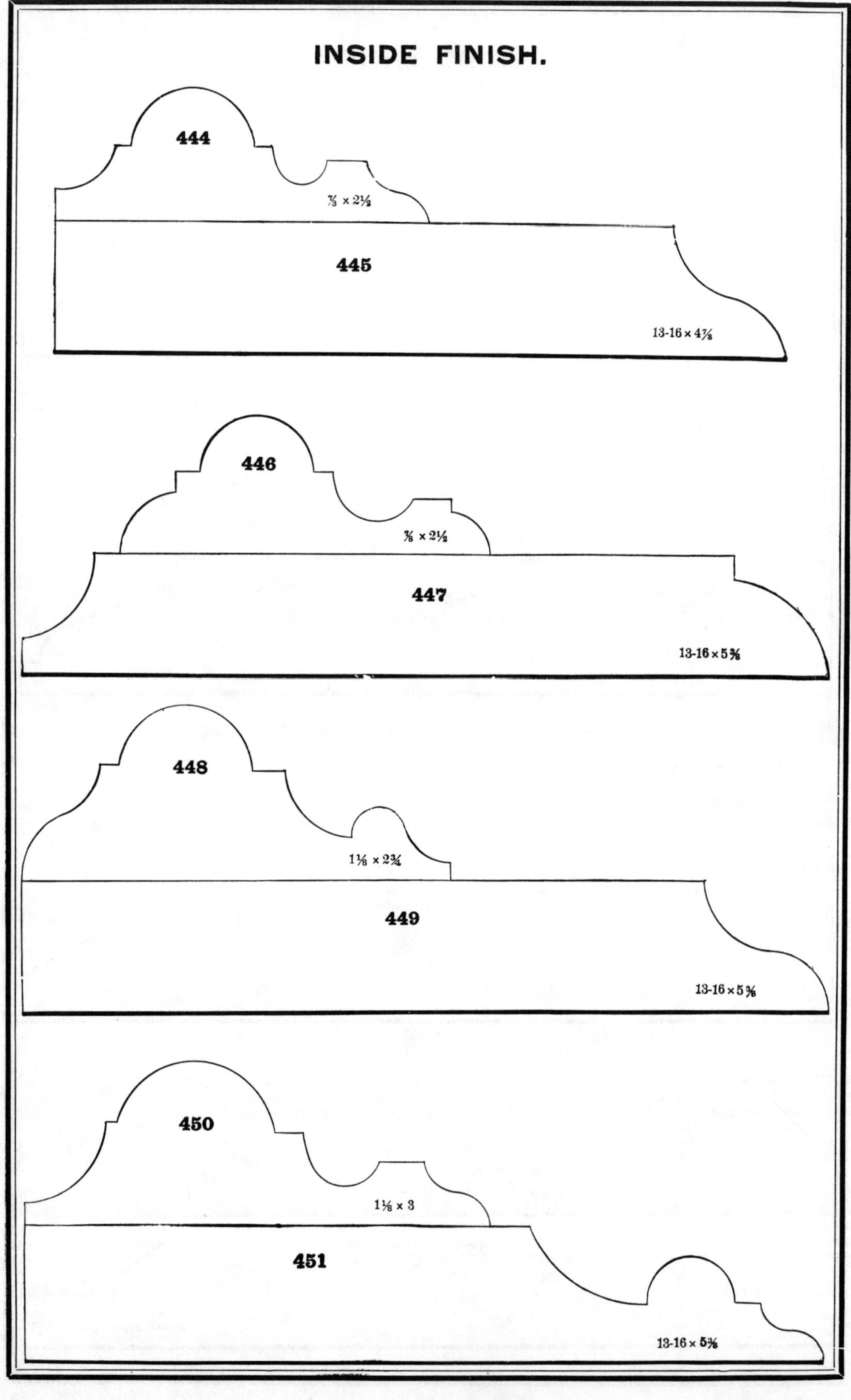
INSIDE FINISH.
444
7/8 × 2½
445
13-16 × 4⅞
446
7/8 × 2½
447
13-16 × 5⅜
448
1⅛ × 2¾
449
13-16 × 5⅝
450
1⅛ × 3
451
13-16 × 5⅜

BASE.

536
⅞ x 3
539
⅞ x 3
537
540
542
544
541
⅝ x ⅞
538
⅞ x 1
543
⅝ x 1
13–16 x 7
13–16 x 7½
13–16 x 8½
13–16 x 7¾

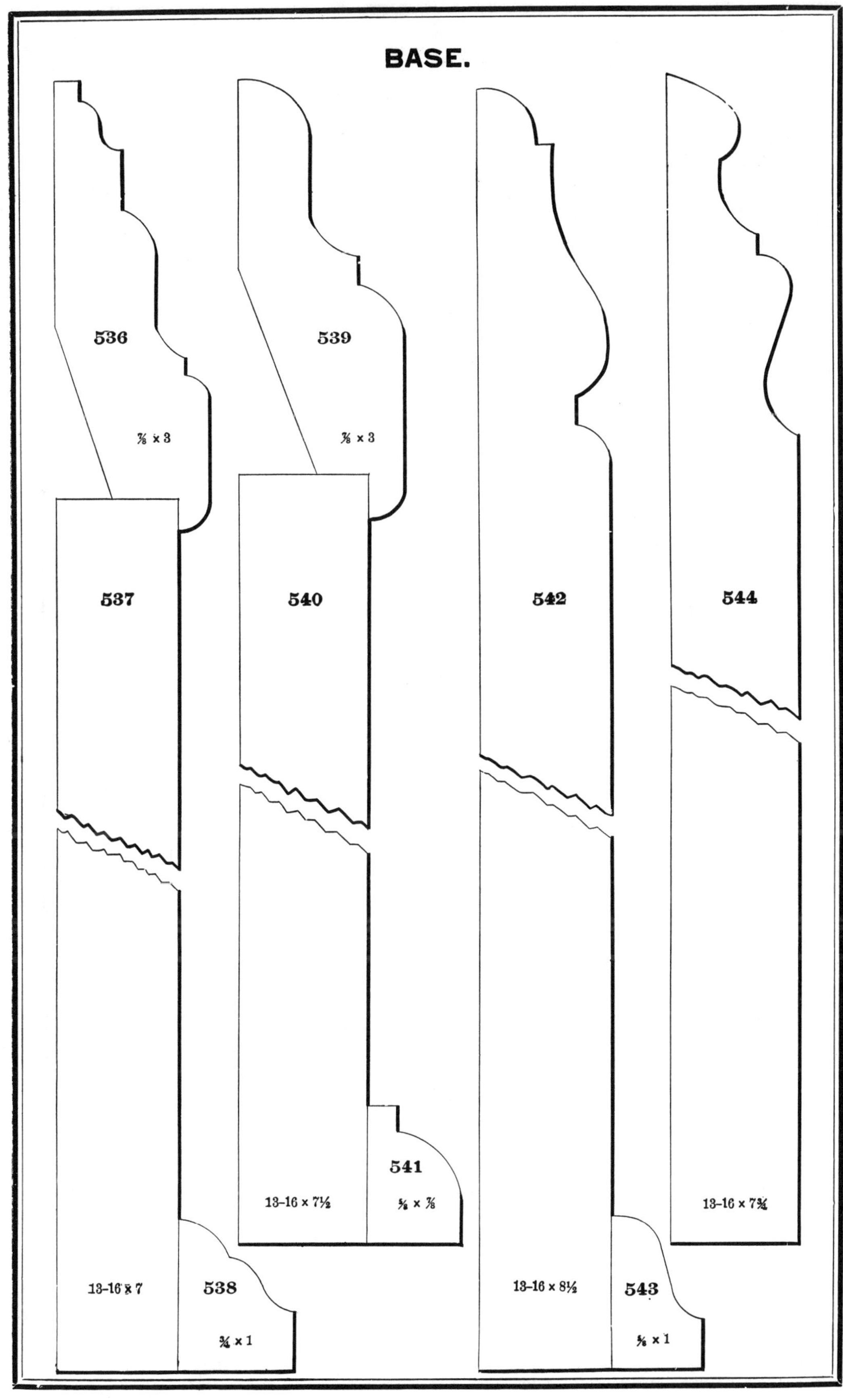

BASE.

526
⅞ × 3¼
527
13–16 × 7
528
⅝ × 1
529
⅞ × 3¼
530
13–16 × 7
531
⅝ × 1
532
⅝ × 3
533
13–16 × 7½
534
⅞ × 1¼
535
13–16 × 7½

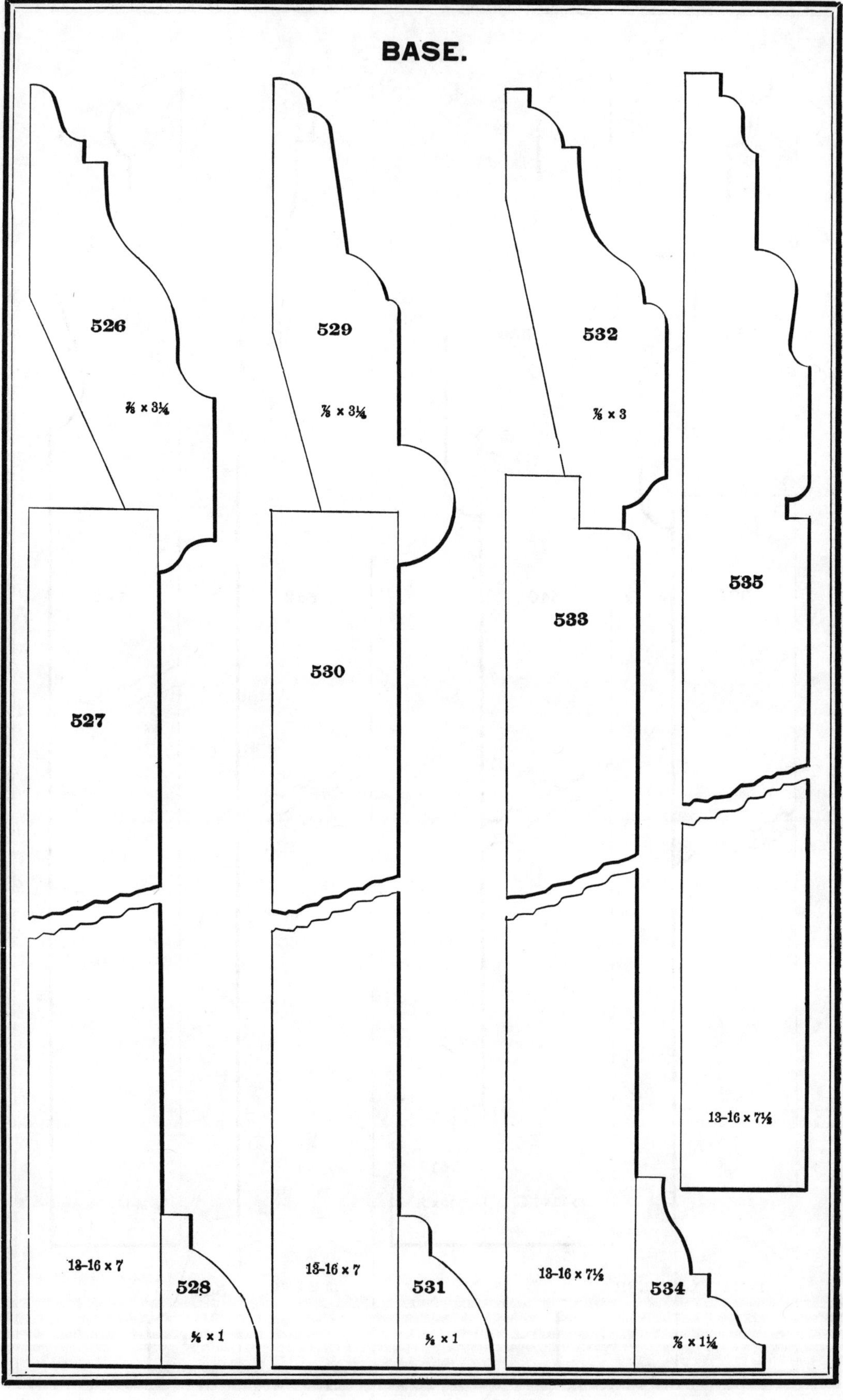

BASE.

483
13-16 × 3
484
13-16 × 7
75
7/8
485
13-16 × 7¼
486
⅝ × 1
487
13-16 × 7½
488
⅝ × ⅞
489
13-16 × 2½
490
13-16 × 7½

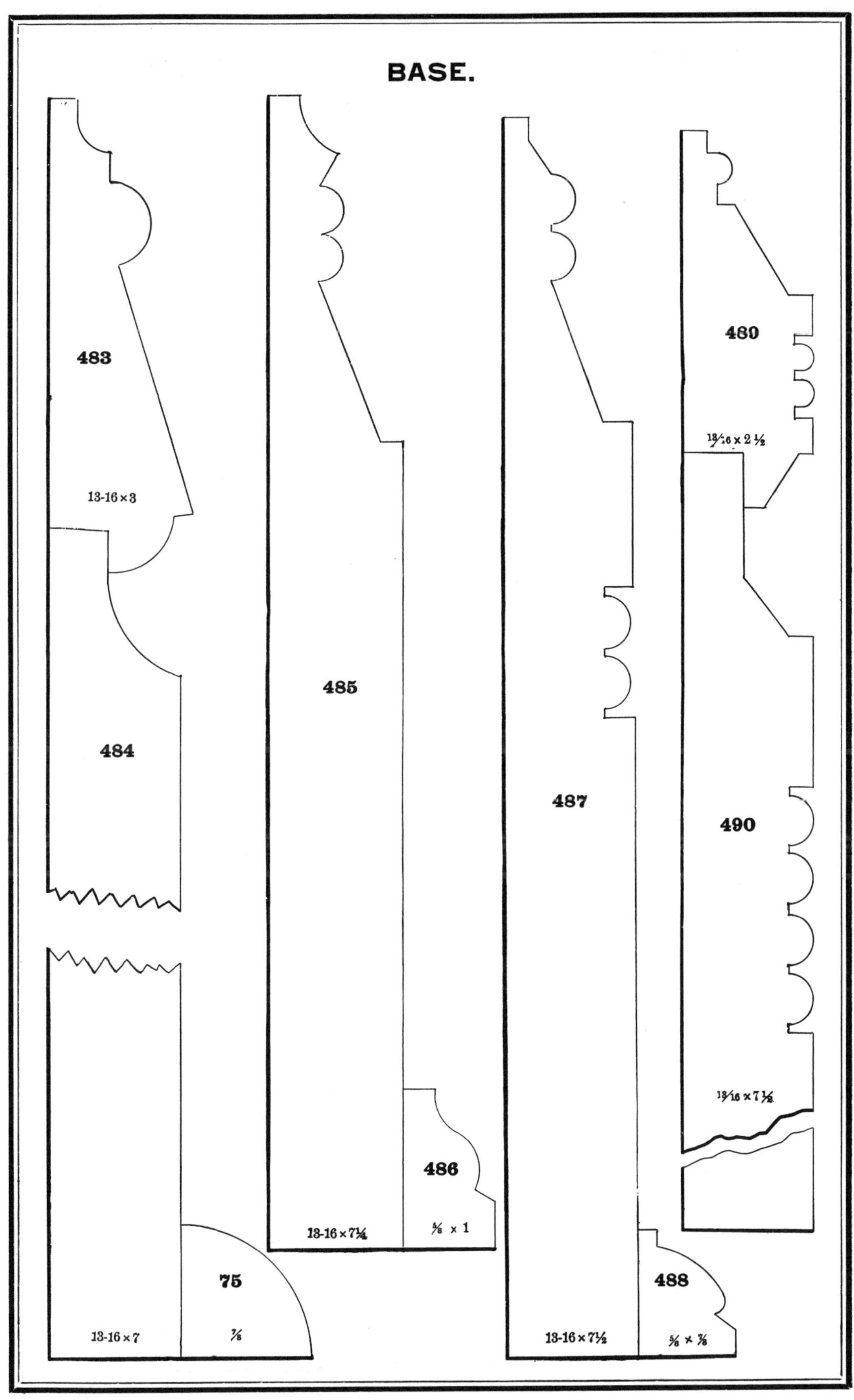

RABBETED PANEL AND BASE MOULDINGS.

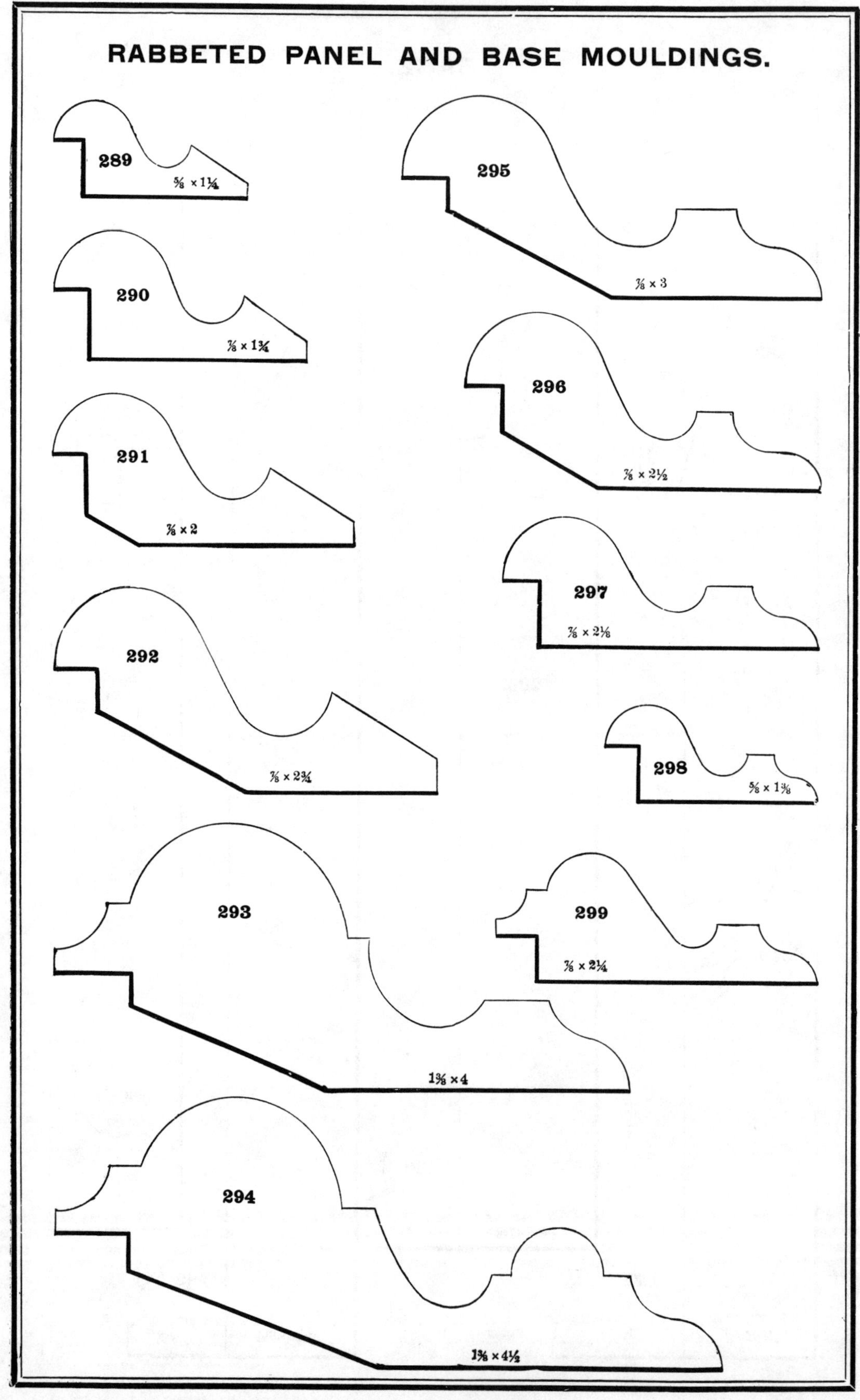

RABBETED PANEL AND BASE MOULDINGS.

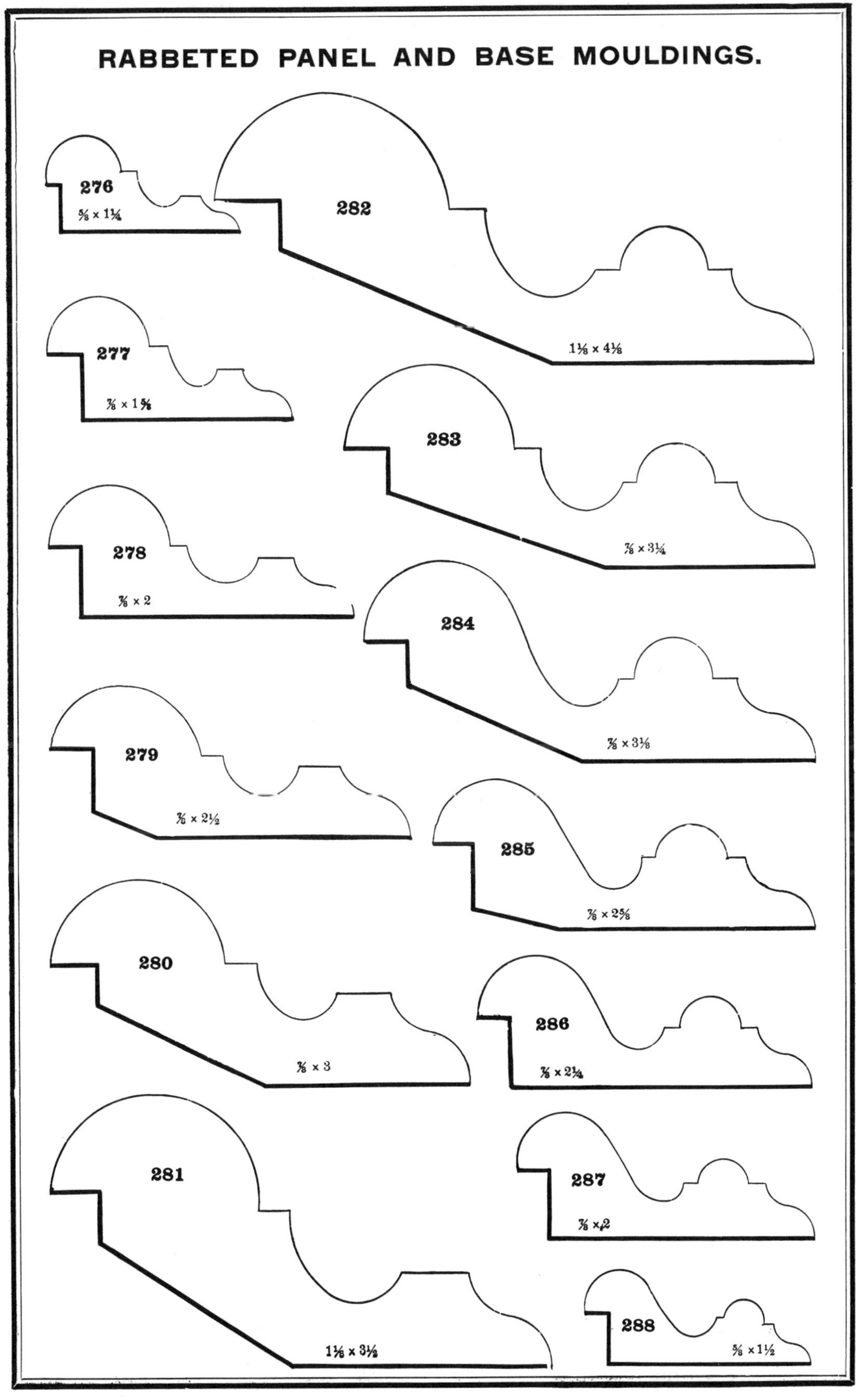

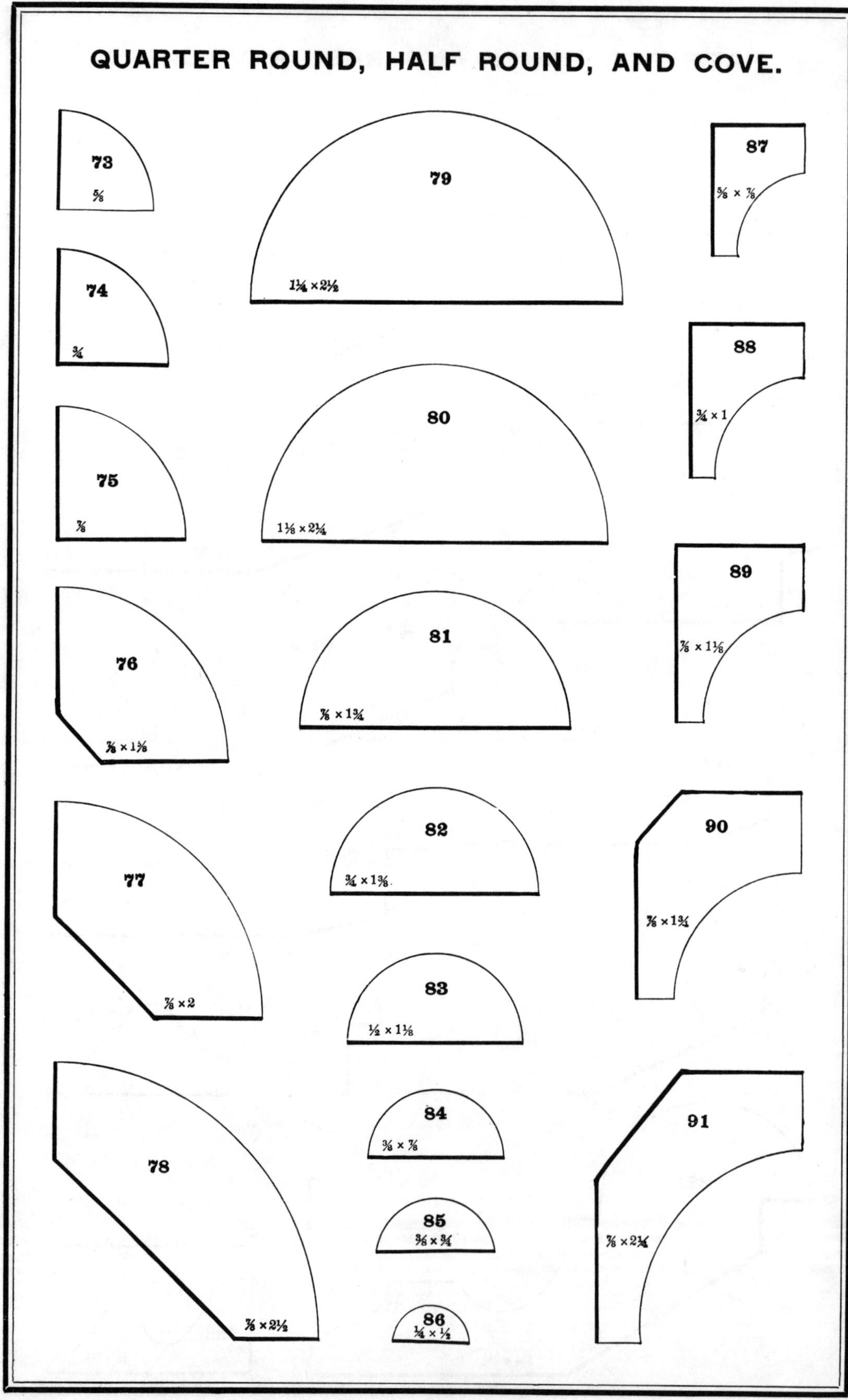

QUARTER ROUND, HALF ROUND, AND COVE.
73
5/8
74
3/4
75
7/8
76
7/8 × 1 3/8
77
7/8 × 2
78
7/8 × 2 1/2
79
1 1/4 × 2 1/2
80
1 1/8 × 2 1/4
81
7/8 × 1 3/4
82
3/4 × 1 3/8
83
1/2 × 1 1/8
84
3/8 × 7/8
85
3/8 × 3/4
86
1/4 × 1/2
87
3/8 × 7/8
88
3/4 × 1
89
7/8 × 1 1/8
90
7/8 × 1 3/4
91
7/8 × 2 1/4

O G STOPS.

91½
⅜ × ⅞
92
⅜ × 1⅛
93
⅜ × 1¾
94
⅜ × 1¾
95
⅜ × 2
96
⅜ × 2¼
97
⅜ × 2½
98
⅜ × 2¼
99
⅜ × 2
100
⅜ × 1¾
101
⅜ × 1⅜
102
⅜ × 1⅛
103
½ × 2½
104
½ × 2¼
105
½ × 2
106
½ × 1¾
107
½ × 1⅜
108
½ × 1⅛
109
½ × 1⅛
110
½ × 1¾
111
½ × 1¾
112
½ × 2
113
½ × 2¼

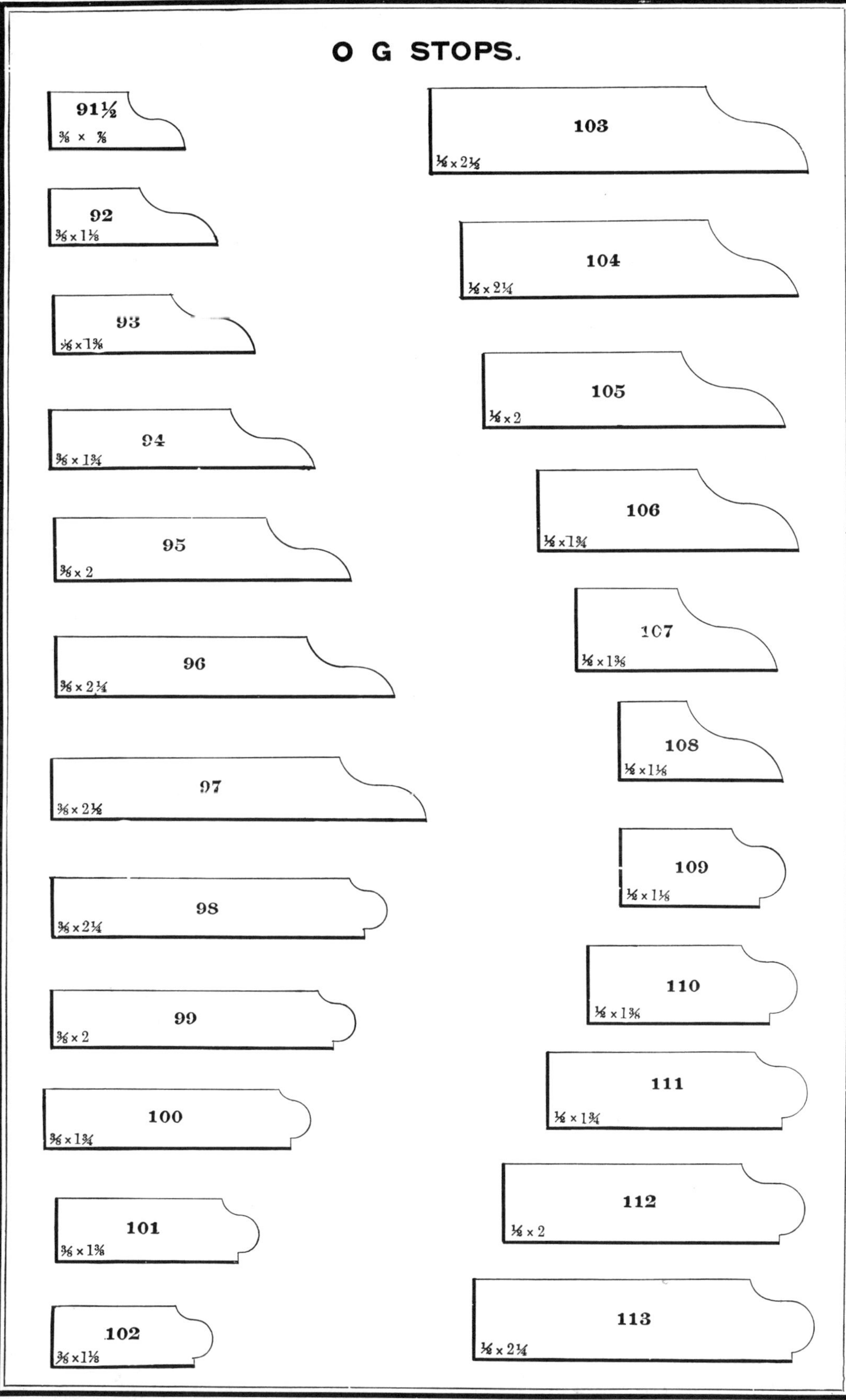

NOSINGS.

153
9/16 × 1
154
3/4 × 1⅛
155
7/8 × 1⅜
156
1⅛ × 1¾
157
1⅜ × 2
158
1¾ × 2⅜
159
1¾ × 2⅝
160
1⅜ × 2⅛
161
1⅛ × 1⅞
162
7/8 × 1½
163
3/4 × 1⅛
164
9/16 × 1

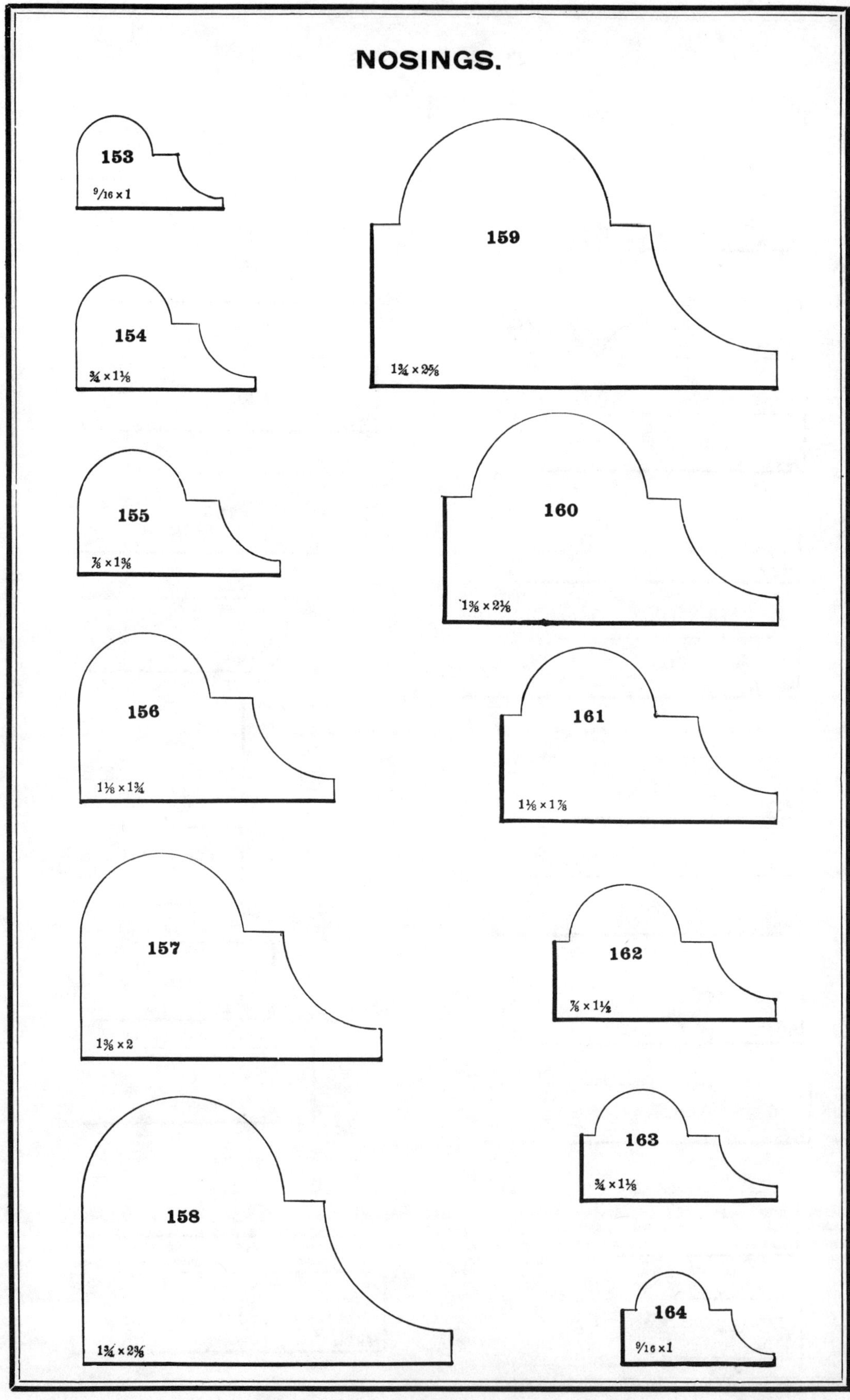

NOSINGS.

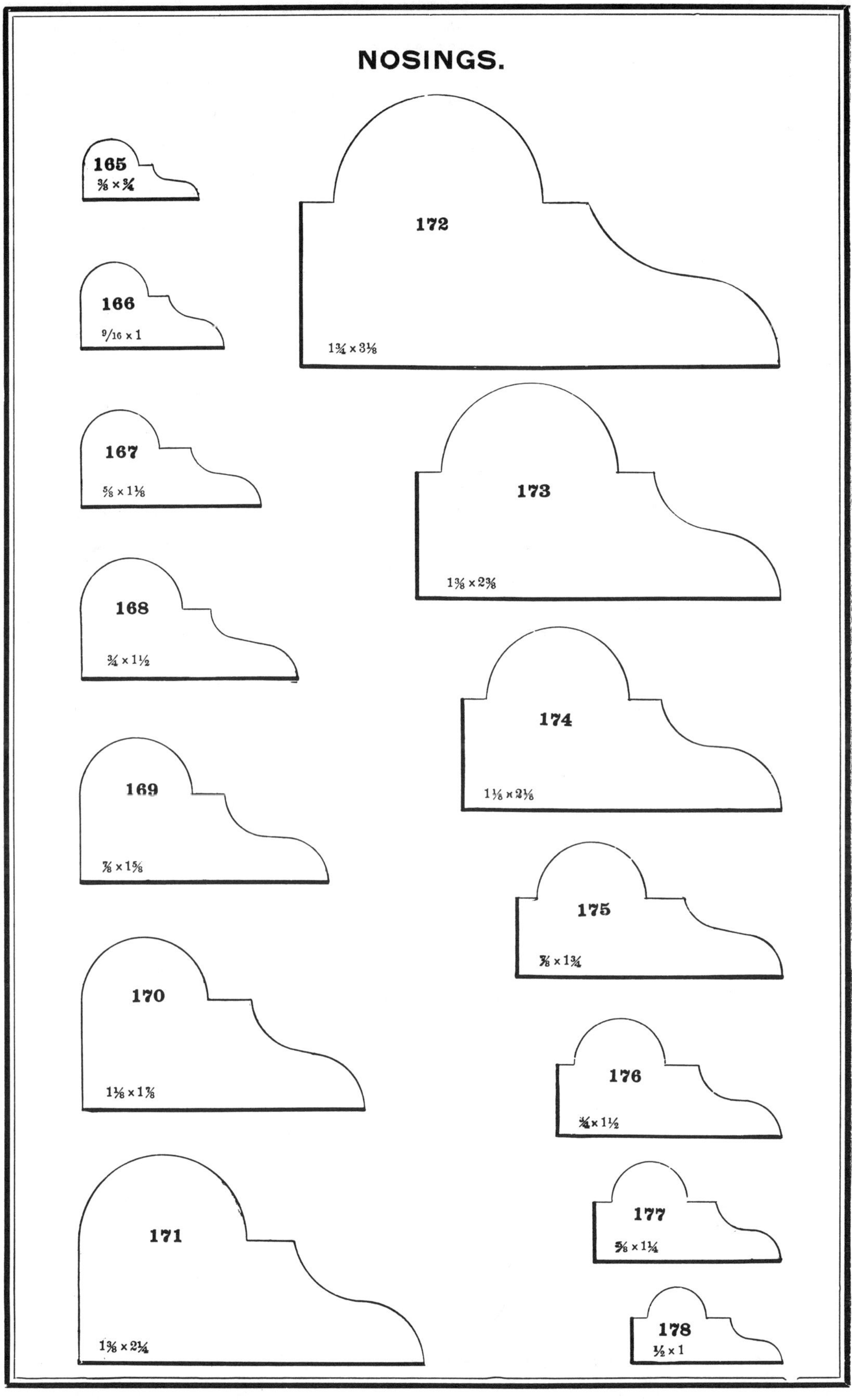

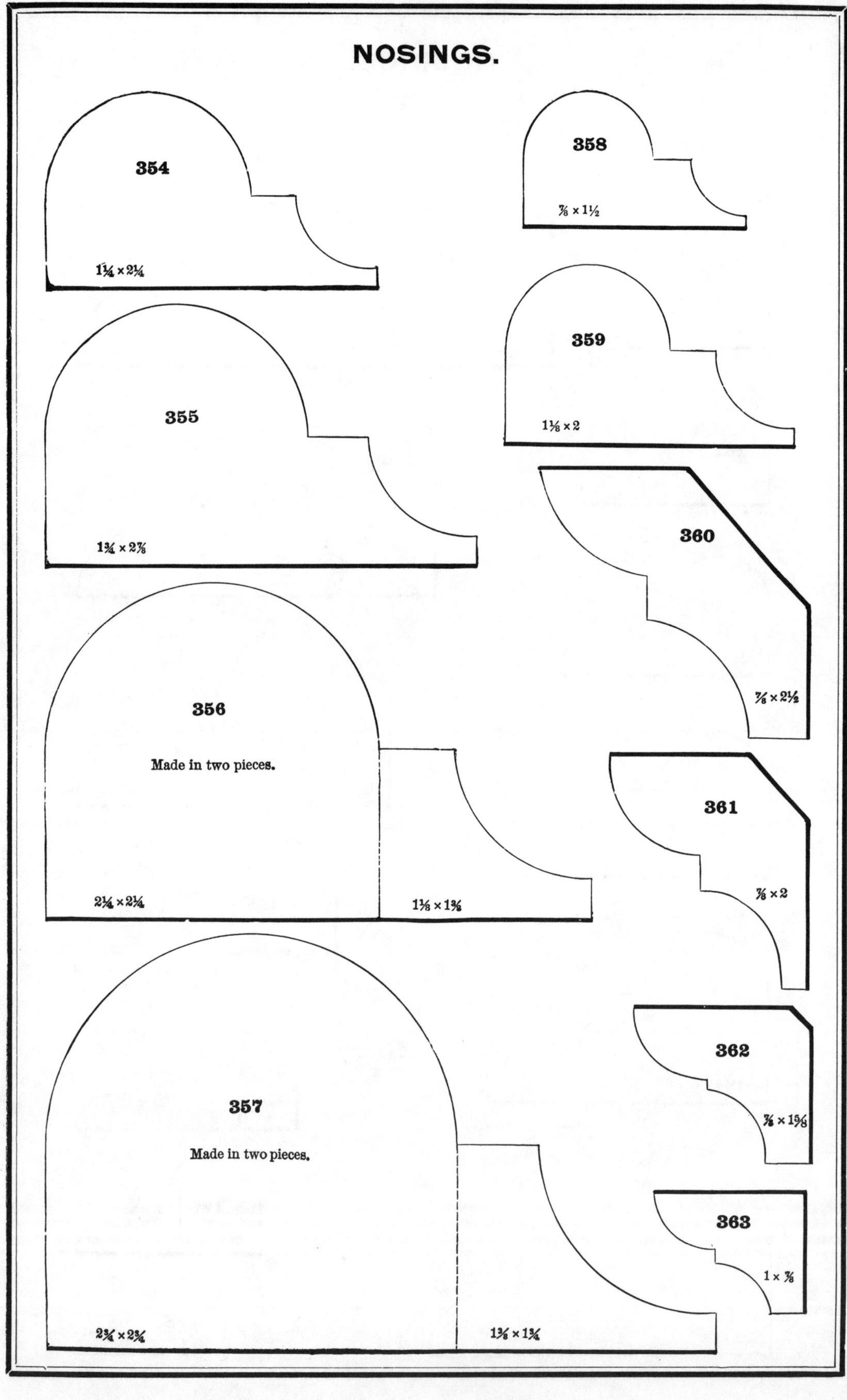
NOSINGS.
354
1¼ × 2¼
358
⅞ × 1½
355
1¾ × 2⅝
359
1⅛ × 2
360
⅞ × 2½
356
Made in two pieces.
2¼ × 2¼
1⅛ × 1⅜
361
⅞ × 2
362
⅞ × 1⅝
357
Made in two pieces.
2¾ × 2¾
1⅜ × 1¾
363
1 × ⅞

PEW BACK RAIL, WAINSCOTING CAP, AND THRESHOLDS.

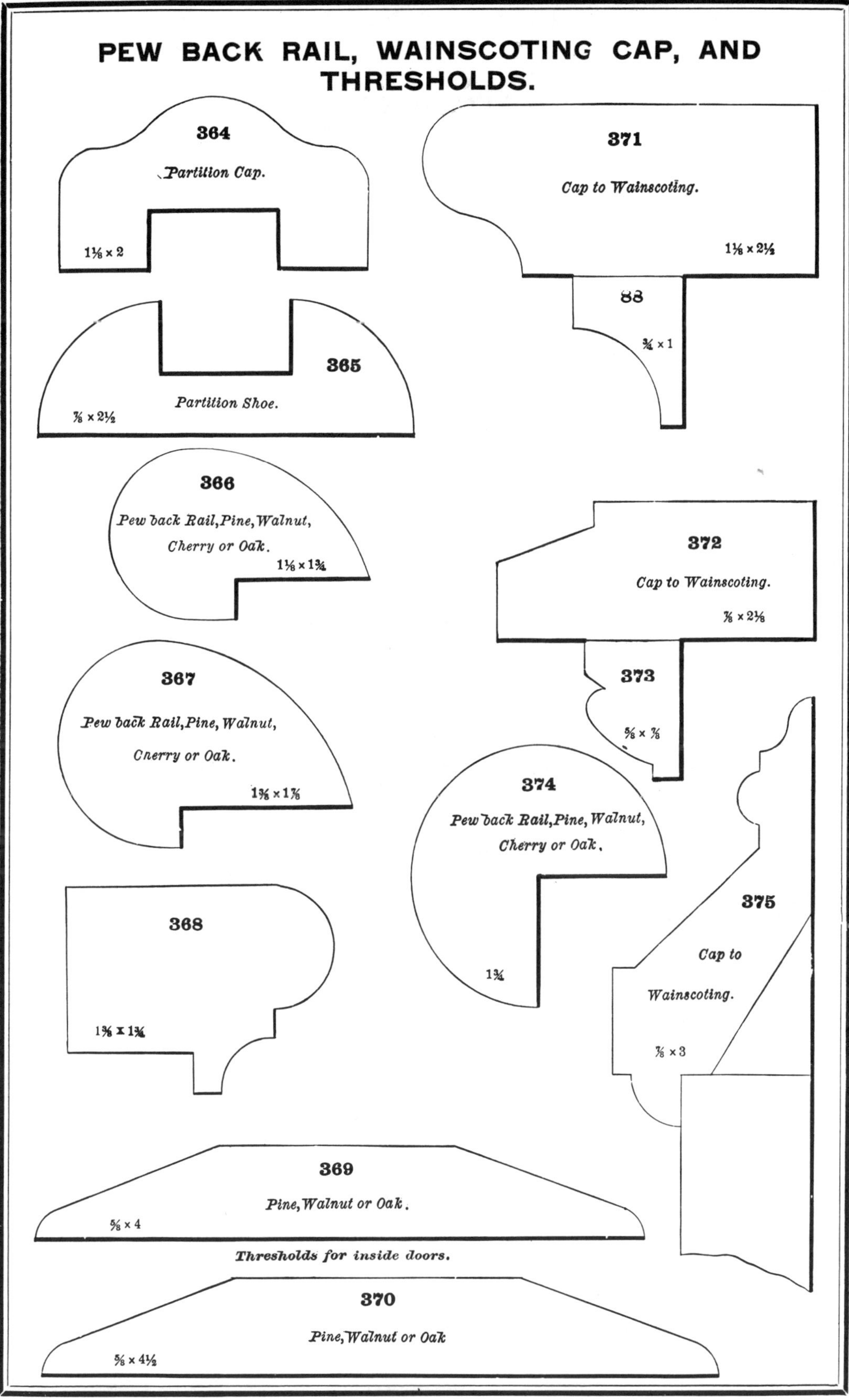

FLOORING.

Flooring; in any hard or soft wood.

491

CEILING.

436

Ceiling or Wainscoting,
in any hard or soft wood.

WOOD VENTILATORS.

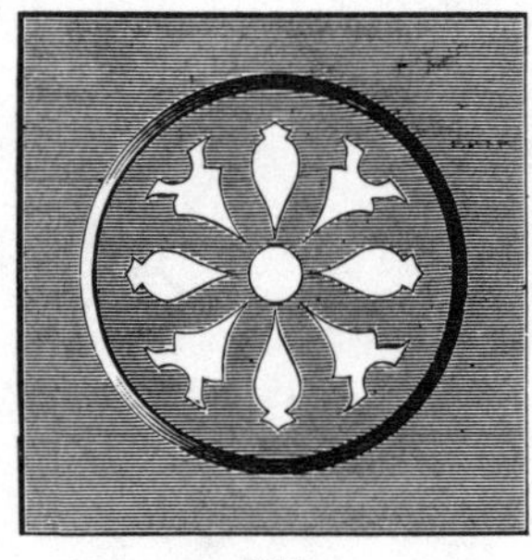

610

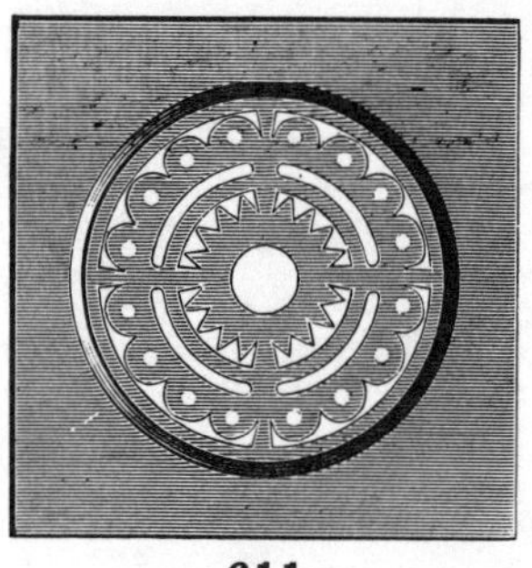

611

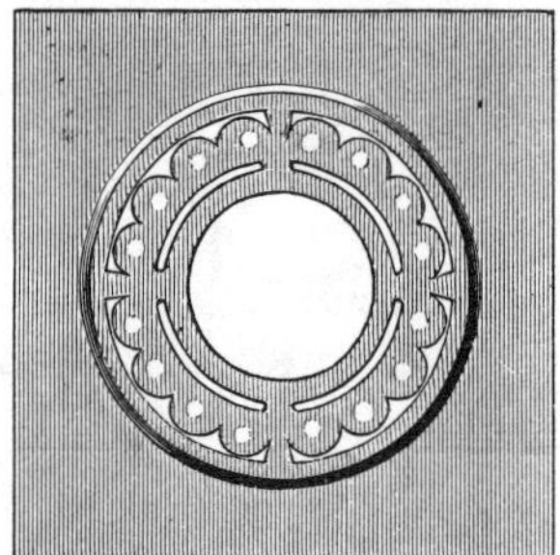

612

INTERIOR FINISHING

Done in Maple, Ash, Red Oak, White Oak, Birch, Cherry, Sycamore, Mahogany, and all other Woods, in the best style of workmanship and of thoroughly kiln-dried material.

ESTIMATES FURNISHED IF DESIRED.

NEWEL.

6